Reflections on the Case for Audit Reform

This is the final volume in a four-book mini series dealing with disruption in audit and financial reporting – this last book focusing on the importance of developing the purpose and concept of auditing in a holistic rather than piecemeal way, whilst reflecting on the case for audit reform.

It looks beyond current events and explores possible new entrants to the market, the role of regulation versus professionalism, developing a more prominent and reinvigorated auditing profession and how to meet wider stakeholder needs. The authors' key proposal for discussion is for the traditional passive audit to be replaced with a proactive style of audit, where granular opinions, forward-looking analysis and sensitivity reviews can aid the reader of accounts to come to their own conclusions.

This book should act as a catalyst for radical thinking professionals, students, academics and company directors to influence future government reforms to meet societal needs in the twenty-first century.

Krish Bhaskar was founding Professor of Accounting and Finance at the University of East Anglia, UK, and previously held positions at the London School of Economics and the University of Bristol. He is the author of more than 50 books and has worked extensively in the IT, consulting, investment banking, automotive and forecasting sectors.

Rod Sellers has spent almost 50 years in senior financial and corporate roles in industry.

Disruptions in Financial Reporting and Auditing

Edited by Krish Bhaskar

Following the global financial crisis and the growing number of major corporate collapses and financial scandals, confidence in the corporate sector, and more importantly, the professionals who audit them, is at an all-time low. Based on the authors' extensive experience and unique research (including interviews with hundreds of professionals, regulators, and whistleblowers) this topical series provides a uniquely accessible insight into the criticisms and challenges currently facing the financial reporting and auditing industry, and examines possible solutions.

At a time of unprecedented scrutiny and technological change, the four complementary volumes critically examine the key debates, drawing on expert opinions from top industry professionals. Together the four volumes combine into an unparalleled contemporary overview and evaluates the future challenges facing this vital part of our economy and society.

Disruption in the Audit Market
The Future of the Big Four
Krish Bhaskar and John Flower

Financial Failures and Scandals
From Enron to Carillion
Krish Bhaskar and John Flower

Disruption in Financial Reporting
A Post-pandemic View of the Future of Corporate Reporting
Krish Bhaskar and John Flower

Reflections on the Case for Audit Reform
Seeking to Avoid Future Financial Scandals
Krish Bhaskar and Rod Sellers

For more information about this series, please visit: www.routledge.com/Disruptions-in-Financial-Reporting-and-Auditing/book-series/DFRA

Reflections on the Case for Audit Reform

Seeking to Avoid Future Financial Scandals

Krish Bhaskar and Rod Sellers

Routledge
Taylor & Francis Group
LONDON AND NEW YORK

First published 2025
by Routledge
4 Park Square, Milton Park, Abingdon, Oxon OX14 4RN

and by Routledge
605 Third Avenue, New York, NY 10158

Routledge is an imprint of the Taylor & Francis Group, an informa business

British Library Cataloguing-in-Publication Data
A catalogue record for this book is available from the British Library

ISBN: 978-0-367-22221-5 (hbk)
ISBN: 978-1-041-03194-9 (pbk)
ISBN: 978-0-429-27386-5 (ebk)

DOI: 10.4324/9780429273865

Typeset in Sabon
by Newgen Publishing UK

Contents

Preface

A passion for learning and a yearning for change

Professor Krish Bhaskar was the instigator and lead author of a series of four books titled 'Disruptions in Financial Reporting and Auditing'. The first three books, with co-author Professor John Flower and contributions from Rod Sellers, were published between 2019 and 2021, but Krish passed away in April 2023 before finalising this fourth book. I have sought to retain the material that Krish had been gathering and analysing in a way that reflects how Krish was framing audit reform priorities, but most of this book was written by Krish before he ceased writing in early 2023. I have added a final, postscript chapter to highlight some key developments up to October 2024.

Krish, born of an Indian father and a white South African mother, studied at the London School of Economics (LSE) before entering academia, teaching at the LSE and Bristol University before being appointed to a founding chair at the University of East Anglia. His academic specialisms were computerised accountancy, audit and all aspects of the use of computers in decision making, including planning, strategy and financial modelling. In total, he published more than 50 books and wrote several hundred articles, papers and monographs.

Amongst his many consulting clients, Krish had a particular professional interest in the automotive industry, starting with research on the prospects for British Leyland and extending to research projects covering many Western car companies.

The subject matter of this series of books felt to Krish like the culmination of all his efforts to bring accountancy into the 21st century technology age, with his emphasis on the great potential for harnessing AI and quantum computing reflecting his undiminished enthusiasm and lateral, forward thinking.

I hope, as Krish did, that readers find that the challenges raised in this book can act as a catalyst for much-needed change in the world of accountancy and audit.

Rod Sellers
October 2024

1 Introduction

This is the final volume in a series of four mini books. It summarises and integrates conclusions from the three previous books and uses these as the basis for analysis of the future of audit and the case for reform.

The purpose of this book is to look beyond current events and have a fundamental rethink of what auditing means and what possible scenarios may be in play in the longer term. The clear intent here is to step beyond short-term remedies and proposals that essentially seek to maintain what can be seen as a rather unattractive status quo haunted by notions of audit expectation gaps – and put on a clean slate the most critical reform considerations and priorities.

The associated website: fin-rep.com

Each book has been published as part of the Routledge Focus on Business and Management, with an accompanying integrated website (fin-rep.com) containing additional material (including appendices and footnotes from the book). Active links are provided for most of the references – meaning that just one click is needed to find introductory or full details of the relevant reference source material. In addition, supporting notes, opinions, and key news items are now contained in one integrated fin-rep.com website (updated to March 2022).

Previous volumes

Some of the main commentary and conclusions of the previous volumes, published between 2019 and 2021, were as follows:

DOI: 10.4324/9780429273865-1

1 *Disruption in the Audit Market: The Future of the Big Four, published, Routledge April 2019*
With the problematic state of the audit market, highlighted by the 'public perception gap', one in four listed audits requiring improvement and prominent concerns about the level of trust in auditors, it was clear to us that something had to change. Some kind of reorganisation of the Big Four appeared necessary but, as of 2019, little change had occurred. The book discussed several radical reforms to the audit market (e.g. audit-only firms, whether the State could run the audit function and, via the FRC, set scale fees, require joint audits, bolster mid-tier challenger firms and use AI to promote/establish an alternative audit service). No single magic bullet to solve the audit market problem was identified but the importance of a will and commitment to change – rather than resolutely defending existing positions – was highlighted and seen as something to pursue actively before the next 'big corporate failure' and associated crisis time for accounting, auditing and corporate governance occurs.
2 *Financial Failures and Scandals: From Enron to Carillion, published Routledge April 2019*
In this book, we analysed the cause and significance of corporate failures and financial scandals involving, inter alia, Lehman Brothers, Enron, Tesco and, more recently and with much publicity, Carillion. The book pinpointed the primary responsibilities of the Carillion board but concluded that many elements of the accounting profession had not served society well – and pointed explicitly to the need for a fundamental reassessment of the purpose of an audit.
3 *Disruption in Financial Reporting: A Post-Pandemic View of the Future of Corporate Reporting, published Routledge January 2021*
We examined financial and corporate reporting and the disruption caused by the 2007/2009 financial crisis, Brexit and Covid-19 coronavirus. Against the backdrop of two major audit tests (i.e. 'truth and fairness' and 'fair, balanced and understandable'), we questioned whether capitalism needed to be re-evaluated and whether there should be greater or reduced regulation (less but better is our response). Hybrid reporting was pinpointed as an important way forward,

combining a relatively brief but very readable 'CORE' report with more detailed 'MORE' reports with the latter also being subject to full audit investigation (designed to do more than just comment when they are inconsistent with the view given by the company's financial statements). With disruptive technologies developing apace through AI and big data/data analytics, we proposed various short-term remedies including more granular or graded audit opinions. To reflect the needs of different users of accounts, we also proposed further use of multiple valuation methods and an emphasis on forward-looking statements, forecasts and projections.

Methodology, pre-requisites and assumed knowledge

The methodology adopted for this volume is summarised in www.fin-rep.com and also see: www.fin-rep.com/wp-content/uploads/book3/Appendix-3.01.2-Pre-requisites-and-knowledge-assumed-for-this-book.pdf.

Primary focus and considerations

This fourth book focuses on the importance of developing the purpose of audit and, through this, a more prominent and reinvigorated auditing profession. It makes direct connection with notions of corporate (social) responsibility and what should be expected of corporations (taking considerable inspiration from issues raised by the 2019 Brydon report[1] and related analysis in academic circles – see Humphrey, 2020a; 2020b; Humphrey et al., 2021; 2024; Knechel, 2021). This, in turn, can extend discussion to other forms of (corporate reported) information that could be utilised and assessed during the audit (not just in terms of being assured or verified but as additional insights assimilated by an audit process intent on helping to build and maintain deserved confidence in the company, its directors and the information it makes public). Consideration is also given to the scope for alternative audit providers, what would reinvigorate competition and choice in the audit market and how corporate reports could develop – and the collective impact of all of this in attracting new students to the field of auditing. Similarly, it is important to assess development possibilities in the functioning of professional bodies and regulators by drawing on assessments of what they have or have not contributed to debates on the future of audit. The nature of government interventions in this area are also considered, especially the scope to have a government appointed auditor for 'hard to audit' companies from which private audit firms (working or not working in the public interest) are refusing to audit. In reviewing government's reform approach, it is important to try to encourage thinking beyond the short term and typically quick fix (but ultimately problematic) reform proposals such as joint or shared audits. We will also consider what we expect from companies in terms of doing more in terms of meeting their corporate social responsibilities (ranging from reporting on their 'public interest' strategies/activities and section 172[2] statement development possibilities to having better boards of directors and more active stakeholder engagement, together with more AGM presence from auditors).

In essence, our recommendations are to choose a central focus and to then utilise different issues, as we do this in terms of scenarios, to relate to development possibilities in our central focus (and to ensure that such consideration of issues/scenarios allow for a connectivity with debates on corporate reporting, accountability, public interest, etc.) The basic spirit is one of seeing audit and its development as a catalyst for advancement in corporate social responsibility and the pursuit of a better society.

Another reason for recommending such a focus is that we can see on several counts that the way the firms are going is to grow other things/services (assurance on ESG, new strategies such as PwCs new equation[3]) by framing them as socially oriented, inclusive, etc. – but this seemingly is leaving audit positioned behind its rather more traditional (limited) parameters.

In 2021, EY took a different stance to revenue growth. The plan, codenamed Everest, caught the world by surprise. EY's global chief was steering a plan to break up the Big Four group that would reshape the oligopoly that has dominated professional services since their rival Arthur Andersen was brought down in 2002 by the collapse of US energy group Enron.[4] Di Sibio and his most senior colleagues weighed a historic separation of EY's audit and advisory businesses after years of criticism over perceived conflicts of interest between the two. Auditors are tasked with holding companies' management to account and resisting pressure to sign off on numbers without proper evidence while their advisory colleagues prefer to keep clients sweet to generate fees in areas such as tax, deals and consulting. 'It surprises me that it's taken this long', says Fiona Czerniawska, chief executive of consulting sector analyst Source Global Research. 'It's becoming increasingly difficult for any accounting firm to offer a multidisciplinary service, which includes audit … I imagine that every other firm is also looking into restructuring'.[5] (*But EY abandoned this restructuring plan in April 2023 due mainly to conflicts between the different partner groups in the USA.*)

This, to EY, had probably been seen as the most effective revenue growth strategy – but it does little if anything (if not, is damaging) to audit professionalism. Audit should be connected much more explicitly to a broader (societal) purpose – this is the type of commitment we should be envisaging for the future/21st century perspective. The current firms' strategies re audit are deeply questionable from a professional perspective ... they are more oriented to 'hole fixing' than 'holistic thinking' as we try to argue.

Disruption in finance

Disruption? The pandemic, the war in Ukraine, Russia becoming a corporate *persona non grata*, the growing dominance of China, Trump's post-truth, and now a worldwide use of fake news, inflation (after decades of price stability), an uncharted and unpredictable commercial world, new trends in finance, the growth (and demise) of SPACs (outside the UK), among a myriad of other commercial and financial events, trends and happenings. And, of course, the overthrown vote winning 'Rock Star' Prime Minister – Boris Johnson. Superimposed on all these issues is a decline of the UK stock market.

For the UK, we have also had to contend with Brexit, evaluated by Rishi Sunak (who was the Chancellor of the Exchequer in 2022) as the cause of a rapid relative decline in our exports.[6] The promised benefits of Brexit seem to be a little illusive. That said the UK must live with where we are at the moment. Never, since World War II, has financial reporting and auditing been subject to so much disruption and change. The effects of supply chain disruption and the war in Ukraine (destroying that country's wheat fertilizer and sunflower oil harvest) have had the knock-on effects of rising food prices and food shortages in the less-developed world. Inflation has returned to the world. The epic fight by Elon Musk to takeover Twitter caused waves throughout the financial community.[7]

This disruption is not just technology-driven but also the combined effect of several factors. These include changing attitudes to openness and transparency, public perceptions, continued corporate failures or what appears to be a misstatement of financial results despite the continuing actions of regulatory authorities. In addition, the auditors continue to give what is in effect a clean bill of health with a crude pass or, occasionally, fail – a black or white stamp despite many shades of grey.

And by the same token one can see plenty of mergers and takeovers. Elon Musk's (Tesla and Space X) takeover bid for Twitter initially valued at $42 billion is testament to this.[8] Fortunes have been made despite the above list of disruption and problems: Asda's private equity buyers (Marylebone-based fund TDR Capital and billionaire Blackburn-based brothers Mohsin and Zuber Issa) recorded a 20-fold return from their debt-laden deal.[9]

Disruption in auditing

This book concerns the external financial audit (hereafter 'audit') and is mainly about the effects of changes in financial reporting and its impact on auditing. In dealing with auditing, we want to examine scenarios for auditing in the longer term. This also has implications for corporate reporting, corporate responsibility and all financial reporting.

Over the years there have been a number of government-sponsored initiatives and publications on auditing and reporting, the most important of which are:

Parliamentary Select Committee into the failure of Carillion[10] (May 2018)

Competition & Market Authority report on the audit market[11] (April 2019)

Kingman Report into the workings of the FRC[12] (December 2018)

Brydon Report into the quality and effectiveness of audit[13] (December 2019)

Arising from the above, there were various Government White Papers and announcements but no legislation to date.

The authors

In this volume, Professor Krish Bhaskar is the lead author with Rod Sellers having sought to pinpoint and integrate Bhaskar's wide-ranging and developing ideas on the subject as they stood prior to his untimely passing. In his career, Bhaskar published more than 50 books and many refereed articles. He also worked in the IT, consulting, investment banking, automotive and forecasting sectors. His practical accounting and business experience included the direct running of companies, preparing financial and strategic reports and different forms of auditing – with his primary specialism being in computer auditing.

Rod Sellers OBE,[14] FCA,[15] has spent almost 50 years in senior financial and corporate roles in industry. He also served as President of the Manchester Society of Chartered Accountants (MSCA) in both 2001–02 and 2022–23 when his role centred on raising the public profile of chartered accountants in the region and initiating discussions on the key challenges facing the audit profession. He is currently a director of MSCA Legacy Limited which utilises funds from the now-defunct MSCA to make awards and bursaries to students and staff at three universities in Manchester to encourage forward thinking of the role of accounting and auditing in the new AI technology age.

Abbreviations

A full glossary of abbreviations and a shortened version are available on: www.fin-rep.com.

Notes

1 https://assets.publishing.service.gov.uk/government/uploads/system/uploads/attachment_data/file/852960/brydon-review-final-report.pdf
2 www.legislation.gov.uk/ukpga/2006/46/section/172
3 www.pwc.co.uk/the-new-equation.html#:~:text=The%20New%20Equation%20is%20an,intelligent%20outcomes%20while%20building%20trust.

4 www.ft.com/content/e3c52090-3a6c-49ea-89b2-022d2d92b076
5 www.ft.com/content/e3c52090-3a6c-49ea-89b2-022d2d92b076
6 Interview with Rishi Sunak during the House of Commons Treasury Committee after a forecast from the Office for Budget Responsibility (OBR) revealed that UK trade with the EU will continue to be down 15% as a result of the country leaving the bloc. Institute of Export, 29 March 2022. Available at: www.export.org.uk/news/600505/Sunak-admits-Brexit-impact-was-inevitable-but-says-government-will-open-trade-with-other-markets.htm. Accessed April 2022.
7 www.thetimes.co.uk/article/musk-raises-46-5bn-in-battle-for-twitter-rszdjkbbt. Then the tech stokes faltered and fell. We believe that Elon Musk found the price too expensive and choose to break the agreement in any way possible.
8 See, for example, www.bloomberg.com/news/articles/2022-04-14/elon-musk-launches-43-billion-hostile-takeover-of-twitter, Accessed April 2022.
9 Asda's private equity buyer records 20-fold return from debt-laden deal, *Financial Times*, 18 April 2022. Available at: www.ft.com/content/c21f0550-4f8d-4ea8-9fba-872eb174ba99, Accessed April 2022.
10 House of Commons. *Business, Energy and Industrial Strategy and Work and Pensions Committees. Carillion.* Second Joint report from the Business, Energy and Industrial Strategy and Work and Pensions Committees of Session 2017–19. HC 769. Published on 16 May 2018 by authority of the House of Common. Available at: https://publications.parliament.uk/pa/cm201719/cmselect/cmworpen/769/769.pdf, Accessed April 2022.
11 Competition & Markets Authority. Statutory audit services market study. 18 April 2019. Available at: www.gov.uk/cma-cases/statutory-audit-market-study, Accessed April 2022.
12 https://assets.publishing.service.gov.uk/government/uploads/system/uploads/attachment_data/file/767387/frc-independent-review-final-report.pdf
13 https://assets.publishing.service.gov.uk/government/uploads/system/uploads/attachment_data/file/852960/brydon-review-final-report.pdf
14 UK Royal honour: Officer of the Most Excellent Order of the British Empire.
15 Fellow of the ICAEW.

2 Audit

What does it mean?

Auditing under scrutiny

In dealing with auditing, we want to examine scenarios for auditing in the longer term. This also has implications for corporate reporting, corporate responsibility and all financial reporting. Auditing can be used in a variety of ways and not necessarily in finance. The common definition is:

> Auditing is defined as the on-site verification activity, such as inspection or examination, of a process or quality system, to ensure compliance to requirements. An audit can apply to an entire organization or might be specific to a function, process or production step. Some audits have special administrative purposes, such as auditing documents, risk, or performance, or following up on completed corrective actions.[1]

Auditing can be applied to anything. In the above case, it applies to quality control: where there can be process audits, product audits and system audits. In the corporate and financial world, we do not have the luxury of such meaningful definitions. Audit has developed over time – often being changed as the aftermath of corporate scandals. Auditing is conducted on entities tasked with the production of accounts. And it has come to be interpreted in a narrow way. Often auditors restrict the word to its statutory meaning. A statutory audit is a legally required review of the accuracy of a company's or government's financial statements and records. An audit is an examination of records held by an

DOI: 10.4324/9780429273865-2

organisation, business, government entity or individual, which involves the analysis of financial records or other areas.

The focus of businesses during and after the pandemic has been on cash and liquidity with an understandable emphasis on short-term survival. This book focuses on the longer term with thoughts of improved agility, flexibility, technology and usefulness in a period where there is a focus on all stakeholders and not just the investors and shareholders. Investors benefit to the extent that they have access to high-quality financial information when making capital allocation decisions. The independent audit, overseen by an active and effective audit committee, is a critical step in providing that information to the capital markets. OCA (Office of the Chief Accountant) staff continue to emphasize the importance of auditor independence in contributing to the credibility of audited financial statements. The staff also recognise the important role the regulatory framework plays in promoting audit quality. When the gatekeepers in the financial reporting ecosystem work together to promote trust and transparency in the quality of information reported for the benefit of investors, our public markets benefit as well.[2]

Audit opinion: pass or fail

This has often been a source of contention. The audit report within a company's annual report has the pass or fail connotation, embedded in the long report will be ' ... have found nothing ...' and so on. Somewhere there will be the statement about the audit opinion. A positive pass will include statements such as: 'the financial statements give a true and fair view of the state of the Group's and of the parent Company's affairs as at xx/xx/xx and of the Group's profit for the year then ended'. Normally there would also be a statement indicating that 'the Group financial statements have been properly prepared in accordance with international accounting standards in conformity with the requirements of the Companies Act 2006' and a statement similar to 'the parent Company financial statements have been properly prepared in accordance with UK accounting standards ...'.

A fail or qualified opinion has implications. These include the possibility of:

1 a fall in the share price and/or substantial boardroom changes
2 a takeover bid
3 the auditor losing this business
4 exposing the entity being audited so that loans/debts are called in and the company fails
5 the difficulty in obtaining all or part of the fees owing to the auditor

Qualifications are rare. There are some incidences where the auditor has not been able to vouch an item and hence may provide an 'Except for' opinion referring to this particular item.

Just trying to google any such opinion and you find examples of what to put in the text but no actual example. That said KPMG set an example by refusing to sign off the 2021 financial results of German real estate group Adler in a rare move that pushed the embattled group into an ever deeper crisis:

> Adler disclosed … that its auditor, who had given the group an unqualified audit in the previous year, would issue a disclaimer of opinion for its 2021 consolidated accounts. 'The auditor has not been able to obtain sufficient appropriate audit evidence to provide a basis for an audit opinion on these annual accounts'.[3]

Indeed, this led to changes in the management of the company.[4] Further developments may occur. Famously, the high-profile Wirecard group failed after EY started investigating missing revenue having given the company a clean bill of health (audit pass). Then, as the FT puts it:

> EY staff began shopping with online merchants identified as clients of Wirecard's Asian partners. The auditors splashed out on a €9.95 seven-day-subscription to an Asian porn site, bought 'coins' for the football video game FIFA 19 worth $23.08, ordered a breathalyser for €33.45 and spent ¥1,000 on bitcoin.
>
> The shopping trip gave a clean bill of health to the Munich-based group – one of many that EY provided to Wirecard during a decade of working for it. Unfortunately, the merchants did not exist. All had been set up by Wirecard executives to

dupe the auditors and help disguise what Munich prosecutors now call 'a fraud in the billions'.[5]

This pass/fail audit opinion was criticized by us in the third volume as being too crude. There should be a more granular approach. We also believe that dwelling on just what has happened is something that needs to change or at least be discussed.

Pivotal events

Let's recap a little. The Global Financial Crisis starting in 2007/8 was a black swan event that changed the course of reporting and auditing for more than a decade. Some well-known pivotal UK failures among many others include:

- Autonomy (2011) – on its sale to HP (Hewlett-Packard).
- BHS (retailer)Considered a financial crisis when it failed in 2016.[6]
- Carillion (outsourcer) See our book 'Financial Failures and Scandals,[7] Chapters 6 and 7 – We concluded that it would be difficult to ignore the company's problems – by management and its auditors (KPMG). The official compulsory liquidation was in January 2018. That said it was more than clear that the group struggled in 2017. However, with hindsight (some would say without) the foundations of the failure were laid several years before.
- BT Group (2017) – accounting irregularities in its Italian business.
- Patisserie Valerie (cakes) failed in 2019.
- Ted Baker (2020) – overstatements.
- P&O Ferries (2022) – some say that this has eroded trust in companies.
- KPMG received the largest UK fine for misleading the FRC/ARGA.[8]
- *(See updates in Chapter 8.)*

The responses:

- Parliamentary Select Committee into the failure of Carillion[9] (May 2018) – where Rachel Reeves (MP[10]) fired some of the worst criticisms ever against the auditing community – much of it well deserved in retrospect (and we agreed with that verdict then).

- Competition & Market Authority report on the audit market[11] (April 2019) – their solution of joint audits (we were against), challenger firms (would take too long) and the operational split of audit from consultancy (now coming about).[12]
- Kingman Report into the workings of the FRC[13] – and proposing metamorphosing into the much more powerful ARGA.
- Brydon Report into the quality and effectiveness of audit[14] (December 2019) – an area we go into in some depth, which we go into later relates to ARGA,[15] created as a result of the Kingman report, and due to be provided with significantly enhanced powers compared to the older FRC. Note once the notion of ARGA (Audit, Reporting and Governance Authority) was published, the FRC ran at an enhanced capacity evolving towards the fully blown and expanded ARGA (even before the appropriate legislation was enacted), presumably with the permission of the then Conservative government (under Theresa May and then Boris Johnson from July 2019 onwards).

Subsequently the Conservative government issued a revised Government White Paper[16] with much of the White Paper to be left to the enhanced FRC/ARGA to implement by way of an enhanced Governance Code for companies.

What is fascinating is that this occurred in 2022/23 and it endows draconian powers on the new ARGA and yet this, in many ways, goes directly against the then government policy for less regulation. The FRC/ARGA appear well able to take on these draconian powers and go beyond the government's remit in terms of company regulation (and red tape). It seems as if the ball is rolling downhill and no one is quite aware that this may be an enormous drag on attracting overseas investment – a cornerstone of the then government's policy (*and now followed by the new Labour government, see links below: the proposed bill* www.morningstar.co.uk/uk/news/AN_1721213926917873400/uk-announces-audit-reforms-to-help-avoid-big-company-failures.aspx#:~:text=The%20new%20bill%20set%20to,company%20Carillion%2C%20which%20left%2030%2C000).

www.accountancyage.com/2024/07/17/labour-government-full-speed-ahead-on-audit-reform/

www.icaew.com/insights/viewpoints-on-the-news/2024/jul-2024/government-can-see-the-economic-sense-of-audit-reform).

Audit reform initiatives and the future of audit

We return to the various suggested audit reforms in the next and subsequent chapters. We are very much driven in this regard by the frequency with which the audit reform initiatives are justified and supported on the basis that they will improve audit 'quality' or better serve society and the 'public interest'; or are accompanied by the importance of ensuring that the 'right' approach is taken or ensuring that we get audit 'right' – but without any expansive consideration as to whether different conceptions of audit could deliver better 'quality', better serve the 'public interest' or are only 'appropriate' in particular circumstances. In short, contemplation of what is 'right' and what is 'quality' are inevitably constrained if we restrict ourselves to one standard conceptualisation of audit or fail to view traditional relationships and statements of position or association from different perspectives and standpoints.

The expectations gap

There has always been an expectations gap about what auditors can do and what the public expect them to do. Theses quotes provide for a description of the issue:

> Although the expectation gap in audit was defined in a number of different ways throughout the years, it is most commonly known as 'the difference between what the public expects from the auditing profession and what the auditing profession actually provides'.[17]
>
> The audit expectation gap arises as a fundamental difference between what the general public expects from auditing and what a financial audit actually involves. In some cases, this gap isn't the result of a lack of auditing knowledge, but more from what the public wishes auditors would do. In either of these cases, there's a gap between expectation and reality.

> The problem with this gap is that it leads to concern about the auditing process in general. One of the most common expectations businesses have is that the auditing process will uncover financial irregularities or instances of fraud in their statements. But this isn't necessarily the role of an audit, which comes with its own limitations. As a result, a business owner might be unhappy that the audit isn't as far-reaching or comprehensive as expected.[18]

However, one of the real issues came to light with the Carillion collapse. This was dealt with in Financial Failures and Scandals: From Enron to Carillion, Chapters 6 and 7.[19] There was clear evidence that the company was in a problem and that the auditors should have known about what were the paper-thin margins on projects that the client was unhappy about and clients may have refused to pay for in whole. Our financial models clearly indicated the company's problems well before the collapse.

Bill Michael (UK Chairman and Senior Partner at KPMG in 2018) in his letter defending the KPMG audit of the 2016[20] said:

> we have no reason to believe that the 2016 Accounts showed other than a true and fair view, and, as we have commented publicly, we believe we conducted our work appropriately and responsibly.

He went on to expand:

> Finally, without seeking to deflect the questions for us that the Carillion collapse rightly raises, it is not correct that an unmodified audit report gives a company a 'clean bill of health'. An audit opinion is an opinion (based on obtaining reasonable assurance) on a company's accounts at a particular point in time, looking back over the previous 12 months, and on the reasonableness of management's view that the company will continue as a going concern for the following 12 months from the date of approval of the financial statements. In some industries, construction being one, an accumulation of adverse developments in specific areas of the business can quite quickly cause a precipitous decline. It does not follow automatically

> from a company collapse either that the opinion of management was wrong, or that the auditor did a bad job.

The problem is that many have pointed out that there was clear evidence and that the auditors bent over backwards to agree management's view of the world which was already far from any possible viewpoint. What Michael did elaborate on was the fact that estimates are often couched as a single number when they are in reality a range:

> Consequently, there is rarely a simple or straight forward answer when considering complex, multi-year contracts, but instead a range of possible outcomes, and, as with any forecast, it will rarely be the case that the actual outcome is exactly in line with expectations. Assigning probabilities to outcomes is highly subjective, particularly if, for example, making a judgement about how a negotiation (for example, in relation to contract variations or penalties) will unfold.

Auditing is often regarded in a repetitive, intransigent nature and has been highlighted in analyses of the audit expectations gap. Houghton et al. (2011),[21] Humphrey et al. (2012) and Adams et al. (2001) are but a few who have analysed the expectations gap. Some may say that this gap dispels the claims that the auditing profession is consistently required to respond to meet ever changing societal expectations of audit. Humphrey (1991) challenged such representations, arguing that the gap is far more static than that, centred historically around similar themes and issues.

Auditing is usually defended in multiple ways:

- We are only required to do what is prescribed by law.
- The role of audit is misunderstood.
- People are expecting more from audit than is legally required.
- Corporate reports have become increasingly subjective and difficult to verify.
- The ultimate responsibility for financial reporting and governance rests with the company's directors
- Collapsed companies are invariably badly run rather than badly audited.

As with the KPMG audit of Carillion, where such a notable corporate collapse might indicate that the audit had been performed to an inadequate standard, it tends to be badged as a one-off event, not representative of the general quality of audit – with attempts made to demonstrate that any such corporate failures are more indicative of failings outside audit rather than within. In fact, in the Carillion case, the FRC announced a formal complaint against KPMG in information provided to the FRC.[22] Accountancy Age reported:

> On January 10, 2022, a tribunal hearing commenced to determine the Financial Reporting Council's (FRC) allegations against KPMG and six of its former auditors. In this article, Andrew Pavlovic, regulatory and professional discipline partner at CM Murray LLP, comments on what is known about the case so far, and the regulatory implications for both the firm and the individual respondents going forwards.
>
> The hearing relates to audit quality review inspections carried out by the FRC into KPMG audits of Carillion in 2016, and Regenersis in 2014. In both instances, the FRC allege KPMG's auditors acted dishonestly and/or with a lack of integrity in creating documents, which gave the regulator the impression more work had been done on the audits than was the case.
>
> The six auditors under scrutiny are of varying experience. Peter Meeham is one of the most high profile; he was the lead partner of the Carillion audit. But several more junior members of the profession, the youngest of whom is 25, are alleged to have been instructed to create backdated documents then provided to the inspectors.
>
> KPMG already conceded in a statement that misconduct occurred, and the regulator had been misled. However, the Big Four firm emphasised the conduct had been self-reported and that such conduct was not systemic or representative of the firm's conduct more generally.[23]

Audit meaning and the public interest

Humphrey et al. (2021) have argued that audit should not be seen as a subset of assurance but the other way round (assurance is a subset of audit). This immediately opens audit up conceptually as audit can be more than assurance (instead of the financial audit being seen as a special or particular form of assurance). Audit can be more than it is and should not allow itself to be trapped in a box, with the profession is defending a fixed but increasingly inadequate conceptualisation of audit.

In terms of the knock-on effects of inflation and the other Black Swan events, we think the fundamental question is how audit is contemplated conceptually – and how willing people are to push its conceptualisation and reach. If you take the Brydon notion of 'helping to build and maintain deserved confidence', then audit can venture into areas that potentially have an impact on how a company and its directors are regarded ... so it becomes a question of what questions you are prepared to embrace as an auditor/or willing for auditors to address and explore. And how you define 'public interest or benefit'. One can raise the notion of an auditor as a social conscience, of someone saying something when others are not prepared to, are scared to do so, or incapable of thinking in that way – they are a voice that speaks when the (public) need is there and/or requires it. What auditors grow up thinking is legitimate for them to comment on is largely socially constituted – you know when you work in an audit firm what you can ask of others (e.g. never ask your audit partner who they voted for in a general election; don't ask people how much they get paid etc.) and learn how to say or do certain things ... and this applies to all dimensions of what shapes 'legitimate' audit work (even the notion that auditors do what they did in last year's file). Some constructions can be seen to be positive, others less so, some normal, some outrageous ... , etc.

Scope of audit functionality

What is a legitimate scope for audit functionality and audit questioning – maybe the trick here is not to answer them definitively but to ask the questions in ways that get people thinking – because much of the above issues takes you back to the basic issue of auditor education ... and the job of an educator (i.e. us) is to analyse, explain, teach, to inspire not indoctrinate. In essence, we have 'to think differently' about audit and encourage others to do so (e.g. see Humphrey 2013; 2019).[24]

We liaise with various people in different activity areas (including public sector auditing and national statistics) and it is clear that many such people are questioning their own roles – for instance, what should the national statistics agency provide in terms of statistics and what should it say when politicians evidently misuse them? Think too of all the questions we have not asked or examined over recent years and what we rely on as accepted accountability mechanisms. What have we monitored and regulated under the Covid pandemic and what have we not/let go/ignored? The government is said by some to have got us through Covid 'successfully' – but 150,000+ people died in the UK … many more (at present) than in some wars … how much money was used wisely or just wasted in schemes for personal protective equipment[25] and to subsidise eating out or furlough? What we audit or do not audit is as we said before socially constituted – and maybe part of the purpose of the book and its role in alerting people to the social significance of auditing and auditing professionalism is that it has to ask uncomfortable questions – the questions that other books don't reach – not least because ultimately that is the central core of auditing – speaking out and asking questions that others don't ask … but also doing or facilitating something constructive through such questioning.

So maybe the selection of questions in the closing part of the book should be designed in a way as to best get people thinking differently about audit – rather than us trying to come up with all the answers. Maybe the really best questions will be the ones to which we don't have ready answers … . For instance, what does public interest really mean … when everyone and anyone is currently claiming (yet continuing to do what they have always done) how much they now work in the public interest.

Impact of the Ukraine-Russian war

This Black Swan event is so important we spend some time in examining its impact on auditing and this raises several questions.[26]

1 It blows a hole in the claims re the capacity of any international financial regulatory system (such as the so-called New International Financial Architecture – NIFA) to deliver

and sustain financial stability – as it is evidently vulnerable to the actions of volatile governments. This also raises questions around the respective responsibilities of business and government and by implication the (social) role and significance of auditing (especially public sector auditing and the capacity of auditors to highlight questionable governmental practices [fat chance?]). If audit (and audit quality) is a social construction (even the FRC acknowledged this in 2006), then what are the limits that constrain audit development – can it never extend to certain areas?

2 Economic consequences of the war – increases in risk exposure for many companies, especially those dependent on geographically distant supply chains and outsourcing arrangements ... questions over the stability of financial statements/balances sheets containing lots of intangible assets/valuations. Presumably will require a heightened focus by auditors on business strategy and assessments of business risk re audited clients.

3 Net zero/ESG[27]/sustainability issues – will not be going away but may be put on the back burner endangering the Earth as we know it. Although the war heightens concerns regarding the fragility of claimed expertise in these areas (e.g. ESG can be almost anything – such that some argue defence stocks are environmentally friendly investments now as such companies help through militarisation to sustain peace). Also highlights the limits of focusing on measurement of ESG/reliance on metrics as against or compared to an emphasis on acting differently – we would like to see more companies taking responsibility for actions rather than a focus on trying to show how good they have been (do it rather than just report it – responsibility has to dominate accountability as the latter can result in game playing with numbers – e.g. we are better nowadays at measuring modern day slavery but it keeps increasing!).

4 We guess the complexity and seriousness of so many issues, conceptually, raises the question as to the role of audit as a catalyst for social change or a barometer on the nature and strength of the corporate world and society more generally ... Is audit a fair-weather function or is it capable of helping significantly when storms are here or appearing on the horizon?

5 In terms of issues of food shortages and famine – the latter has existed in some parts of the world and not had a significant impact on things like NIFA (or NIFA's representation of ways of addressing it – such as capacity building efforts in relation to the global strengthening of professional accounting bodies – has been conceptually inadequate/peripheral ... such that we have been kidding ourselves when claiming that we have a more stable world). So, will they do so now? Will they demand/require major social change and different government and corporate action (and by implication, different forms of auditing)? We guess much depends here on social outlook and philosophies and what you define as a just and fair world? It certainly questions the strap lines of the Big Four when they talk of building a better working world as to how far they are prepared to push and pursue this ... and how stuck or flexible are conceptualisations of audit, risk, accountability, responsibility, etc.

Getting bogged down in detail

In stepping back from some of the details of the individual cases and reports, we have to think how best we could incorporate a book on audit that takes in a thematic approach.

In this regard, there seem to be a host of recurring problems and failings associated with sudden corporate collapses and questions about the quality of audits prior to any such collapse or evident major undetected fraud. We could seek to categorise these in more specific/individual detail (e.g. a problem of accounting reports insisting on point valuations rather than indicating the likely range of acceptable values; or an evident lack of auditor scepticism or insufficient forensic focus; or the making of basic mistakes; over-domineering company management; remuneration and bonus structures creating or incentivising inappropriate behaviour; a market for audit services that systemically leads to an under-pricing of audit fees, etc.). Or we could choose to treat them under a more generic heading such as 'recurrent events or failings' and connect these with other reasons/themes as to why it is important to try to reconceptualise or think differently about audit etc. We quite like the latter approach as we think it allows us to more creative/imaginative. For instance,

Carillion seems to be revealing all sorts of not so actively discussed issues around the nature of the working environment and culture within Big Four firms (which is in need of more analysis – especially in terms of what it means and implies re ruling notions and conceptualisations of accounting and audit 'professionalism' and a way of problematising some of the claims made by Kieran Poynter at PwC[28] regarding regulation making audit recruitment more problematic. The pursuit of a new auditing standard for auditing less complex entities (LCEs) – currently at the exposure draft stage – is another area where there is a potentially big opportunity to reconceptualise audit but this is likely to get lost with the new standard basically being a slimmed down version of existing ISAs.

We could see such broader-based themes offering a quite persuasive case for us in this book to start to advocate where conceptual development ('purpose-based' reform) could be best pursued. It is also an approach that we could use to assimilate what we have already established in the three previous books – setting a stage or platform, in essence, to lay out the policy reform and intellectual agenda for this book.

The profession versus regulation

Another big theme would be the relationship between the profession and regulation (and also the relationship between professional bodies, regulators and the big accounting firms). This has already been touched upon when the FRC's published its tighter control of the RSBs (Recognised Supervisory Bodies) and the audit firms.

Likewise, the relative emphasis attached to regulation and markets as compared to professionalism. Establishing these as core themes would allow for the type of reflections that we are providing regarding the frequency of regulatory reports/publications and what to do with regulatory fines and how, for example, they are treated by firms. We stress that independent audit regulation is not building higher levels of confidence in audit, but we accept that the regulators keep finding failings which themselves raise questions about ruling levels of professionalism and the nature of the working environment in audit firms.

We also see frequent examples of the profession acting in ways that seem to prioritise standard setting processes over the enhancement of professionalism (such as arguments that we need to promote global standards and convergence to global standards ... almost regardless of any analysis of their relative quality ... and need to know what the regulator will accept or buy into when firms or institutes are framing their reform proposals and responses to 'calls for views').

ICAEW's power relative to that of the FRC/ARGA

The loss of control by the RSBs and the greater authority of the FRC/ARGA was first flagged up in the Kingman report (see recommendation 15, page 29):[29] It is also worth reading parts of the Kingman report where it discusses the nature of RSBs (Recognised Supervisory Bodies) and also its views on the effectiveness of regulatory oversight (e.g. pp. 44–45). This whole issue seems to have received very little attention in the press – and for us it is particularly puzzling as to why the ICAEW did not challenge this and instead expressed support for the establishment of a strong regulator.

If you search for the word 'professionalism', it does not appear once in the Kingman report. The professional bodies should have picked this up. A big theme for us is whether regulation is bolstering or hindering professionalism. We doubt that regulatory action is restoring confidence in audit. We seem to be quite close to the circumstances at the time of Enron and/or the global financial crisis. Although, it could be argued that it is different in other countries.

The Kingman report called for greater working together with the Insolvency Service – so that the focus would start to shift from punishing errant auditors to punishing errant directors – but even here the Kingman report was still fairly cautious on the issue of director disqualification (we think what the ICAEW et al. mean when they speak of a strong regulator is that they want a regulator that is strong against errant directors – but it is also going to be strong in terms of its dealings with the profession – but in our view a strong profession does not need a strong regulator). This was also suggested by the Kingman report.[30]

Notes

1 What is an Audit? – Types of Audits & Auditing Certification. Ages & Stages Questionnaires website. Quality resources. Available at: https://asq.org/quality-resources/auditing#:~:text=Auditing%20is%20defined%20as%20the,%2C%20process%2C%20or%20production%20step. Accessed April 2022.
2 Paul Munter, The importance of high quality independent audits and effective audit committee oversight to high quality financial reporting to investors. 26 October 2021. Available at: www.sec.gov/news/speeches-statements?aId=edit-news-type&field_person_target_id=&year=All&speaker=&news_type=Statement. Accessed April 2022.
3 www.ft.com/content/bab94fc9-1d70-4d6a-93dd-642853fee677
4 Adler Board Members Quit After Auditor Refuses to Sign Off on Huge Loss, Bloomberg, www.bloomberg.com/news/articles/2022-04-30/adler-posts-1-24-billion-loss-in-report-auditor-won-t-endorse
5 www.ft.com/content/bcadbdcb-5cd7-487e-afdd-1e926831e9b7
6 https://committees.parliament.uk/committee/164/work-and-pensions-committee/news/98027/leadership-failures-and-personal-greed-led-to-collapse-of-bhs/
7 Bhaskar, K. et al. Financial Failures and Scandals: From Enron to Carillion. Routledge April 2019.
8 www.ft.com/content/ef2c5ff2-bada-4ffc-8900-4a74e9d8c7a3
9 House of Commons. *Business, Energy and Industrial Strategy and Work and Pensions Committees. Carillion.* Second Joint report from the Business, Energy and Industrial Strategy and Work and Pensions Committees of Session 2017–19. HC 769. Published on 16 May 2018. by authority of the House of Common Available at: https://publications.parliament.uk/pa/cm201719/cmselect/cmworpen/769/769.pdf Accessed April 2022.
10 On the Opposition's front bench as Shadow Chancellor of the Exchequer in 2021.
11 Competition & Markets Authority. Statutory audit services market study. 18 April 2019. Available at: /www.gov.uk/cma-cases/statutory-audit-market-study, Accessed April 2022.
12 https://assets.publishing.service.gov.uk/media/5d03667d40f0b609ad3158c3/audit_final_report_02.pdf
13 https://assets.publishing.service.gov.uk/government/uploads/system/uploads/attachment_data/file/767387/frc-independent-review-final-report.pdf
14 https://assets.publishing.service.gov.uk/government/uploads/system/uploads/attachment_data/file/852960/brydon-review-final-report.pdf

15 https://assets.publishing.service.gov.uk/government/uploads/system/uploads/attachment_data/file/767387/frc-independent-review-final-report.pdf
16 www.gov.uk/government/news/audit-regime-overhaul-to-help-restore-trust-in-big-business
17 www.accaglobal.com/in/en/professional-insights/global-profession/expectation-gap.html
18 https://gocardless.com/en-us/guides/posts/what-is-expectation-gap/
19 Financial Failures and Scandals: From Enron to Carillion, Routledge, 2019.
20 www.parliament.uk/globalassets/documents/commons-committees/work-and-pensions/Correspondence/Letter-from-KPMG-Chairman-to-the-Chairs-relating-to-Carillion-2-February-2018.pdf
21 https://openresearch-repository.anu.edu.au/bitstream/1885/35292/2/01_Houghton_Materiality_in_the_context_of_2011.pdf
22 www.frc.org.uk/news/september-2021/frc-announces-formal-complaint-against-kpmg-and-ot
23 www.accountancyage.com/2022/01/28/an-update-on-kpmgs-carillion-and-regenersis-misconduct/
24 https://snsse.cdn.triggerfish.cloud/uploads/2020/02/2014-01-30_thinking_differently_-_making_audit_innovation_the_new_practice_standard.pdf; https://auditfutures.net/blogs/thinking-differently-is-audit#:~:text=Christopher%20Humphrey%20is%20Professor%20of,public%20expectations%20of%20audit%20practice.
25 www.independent.co.uk/news/uk/politics/ppe-waste-nhs-spending-report-b2005093.html
26 See also www.icaew.com/technical/audit-and-assurance/audit/guide-to-auditing-implications-of-war-in-ukraine
27 ESG stands for Environmental, Social and Governance. Investors have been increasingly applying these non-financial factors as part of their analysis process to identify material risks and growth opportunities as stated earlier.
28 Interview: PwC Chief – Poynter's progress | Accountancy Daily, January 2022.
www.accountancydaily.co/interview-pwc-chief-poynters-progress
29 https://assets.publishing.service.gov.uk/government/uploads/system/uploads/attachment_data/file/767387/frc-independent-review-final-report.pdf
30 Recommendations 36, 37 and 38 of the Kingman Report.

3 Audit industry issues and problems

In investigating possible answers to the questions of 'How do we make auditing a positive and progressive force for good?', we thought we should examine the current state of auditing. After all the new definition of PIE and the increasing regulatory control of many more audits leaves the audit industry in a new state of flux. We should remember that audit firms are businesses and they have encountered massive changes since we first volume 1 of the four books. This represents some of the current issues engulfing audit firms,

Audit firms' major issues: staff shortages

The continued mantra among the accounting firms is the same: 'we are sold out', 'there are not enough accountants', 'Can't attract graduates', 'not enough qualified accountants' 'can't keep our qualified staff' and so on. That leads firms not wishing to take on any audit work that might be considered at all risky – due to the reputational risk and added to by the firms' strong criticism of the retrospective and non-supportive attitude of the FRC/ARGA.

Kevin Ellis, former head of PwC UK, believes the audit profession is still attractive to new recruits but retaining qualified staff is becoming an increasing issue. PwC say its attrition levels for recently qualified auditors were significantly higher than in other parts of its business in 2022, and higher than previous years. This trend is reinforced by other input and reports from the accounting and audit profession.[1]

DOI: 10.4324/9780429273865-3

Structure of audit firms and outsourcing

The Big Four are also seeing a more cylindrical rather than pyramid structure to their audit teams as routine testing is devolved to more technology processes and a much greater reliance on the outsourcing of work to offices based in developing countries. However, although they are still finding it possible to recruit high quality graduates, the cost of training means they are becoming uncompetitive (re salaries) versus investment banking, legal, etc. The firms, including now BDO and Mazars (who have both taken on more clients recently), are now fully resource stretched and struggling to take on more work – hence reducing competitiveness and generating the problem of companies not having a great deal of response/choice when opening up their audit to tender processes.

Professional staff and trainee shortages

The Big Four would argue that the negative reaction to the scandals from Carillion onwards seems to have adversely affected recruitment and, especially, the accounting firms' ability to retain professionally qualified staff. That is not the whole story because we maintain that the trainee salaries (less than £30,000 usually) and qualified staff (less than £60,000) are no match for the IT, banking, medical or legal professions. GPs can easily earn well over £100,000 for fulltime work and possibly much more.[2] More importantly, entry level salaries for technology companies are substantially higher and can after a few years reach to well over £100,000. In these terms the accounting profession is not paying enough compared with comparative professions. (Meanwhile the top tier partnership level is earning close to £1 million per year[3]). In addition, the negative impact of the bad publicity leads to a drain of qualified staff away from accounting firms to where their skills are sought after and rewarded in higher salaries, less personal risk/public rebuke and other benefits.

We find the argument that accounting salaries are high enough to be less than persuasive and personnel have made their disagreement felt in terms of walking away from the accounting and auditing professions.

In other anonymous conversations with the Big Four and other audit firms, we have found that they are all under pressure. They cannot fulfill all the work offered to them. They are turning away work.

An audit firm's view

Mazars, one of the firms just outside the Big Four, made a member of comments when interviewed about the auditing reform bill. Bob Neate (partner in Mazars leading UK audit) commented to Accountancy Age:

> I do not know of a major firm that is not feeling capacity constrained at the moment. Every firm is struggling to resource and perform the work being requested of us. And we are all having to turn away work that, a few years ago, we would have loved to do.[4]

Adding significant additional burden, as the audit reform bill will do, on audit firms who are still working through the legacy of Covid-related delays and the inefficiencies of remote working creates challenges and potentially quality risk. Neate of Mazars goes on to say:

> Our teams, in truth, are tired, because we've been working incredibly hard for a very long time. And that's what I mean by we're overheated at the moment. There's more audit work being required than the profession has the capacity to deal with.
>
> With that in mind, if you bought in a lot of additional burden in the next year or so, something could break or companies will not find an auditor. And that's the risk. Having a little more time to continue to build resource is helpful. However, that shouldn't be a reason for not moving forward, because it's important to the whole ecosystem that the reform packages come through.[5]

Public Interest Entity (PIE)

Another area requiring more auditor resource is for Public Interest Entities. There is however much concern over the current definition. In fact, submissions to the BEIS emphasised the need to have more nuances in deciding how to define a PIE – size alone is not necessarily the key factor but more, as the name suggests, what is actually 'a public interest company' in terms of its products or operations and implications for the country. This impacts how to identify such companies and the effect on the auditor's responsibilities for a regulated company.

Neate likes the delay before enacting the audit reform legislation and he also liked the fact that fewer companies would come under the PIE umbrella – the estimate is that the reforms will sweep just 600 more private companies into the tighter regulatory system, compared to an original plan to potentially double the number of so-called 'public interest entities' to as many as 4,000.[6] Neate said:

> it comes back to this market capacity point – you do have to do more work for anything that falls within the PIE range. So broadly, I think not going over the top makes sense.

Capacity constraints is something that the audit industry is grappling with. This applies not just to new recruits but also qualified staff across the entire range of experience.

Reason for staff shortages

A growing audit business as the nature and scope of audit widens. Recruitment not keeping pace or, if anything, going backwards. These two issues cause a major problem. That is before we expand the audit scope with the new regulations and before we add another 600 companies requiring audits under the new PIE regulations which now includes private companies.

> A core issue is actually that people just aren't there to recruit, or at least not in the numbers we all collectively need. Our audit business grew 30% last year, and that means our headcount needs to grow at 30%. Finding those additional heads in this market is very difficult. As a global firm, we've done that by drawing upon our resources from around the world, and that works okay, but it's not the ideal long-term solution.[7]

Brexit has not helped as the audit firms cannot draw upon their European counterparts so easily:

> I have to say, Brexit hasn't helped. We've got a very significant European presence as a firm, and it's not as easy to bring people across anymore – there's a whole new level of bureaucracy and cost attached now.[8]

And a final word on trained staff shortage:

> The volume of work as a whole has grown, but the number of people that exists as qualified, experienced accountants hasn't grown at the same pace. We're all trying to remedy that by taking on significantly more trainees. We're looking to take 350 this year. But of course, it takes three years to train to qualification and we need experienced talent now. It is that conundrum of getting enough heads to cope with the growth opportunity, but also being conscious of not growing too fast because you need to bring people in and train them to our ways, and that takes time.[9]

Other current audit issues

Institutions have, in the last few months, begun writing to auditors (not companies as far as we know) asking for more reassurance on especially the ESG (Environment, Social and Governance) and climate control risks/reports. They believe that many users, perhaps mistakenly, believe that everything in the Annual Report is 'assured' and hence they are looking for auditors, either directly or via separate expert reviews, to give positive affirmation rather than the current weak 'nothing materially at variance with the financials' comment. We believe this suggests a more robust approach to the soft sections of the annual report will develop with auditors content to be involved but clearly delineating their responsibilities.

Auditors currently and increasingly refer to other sections of their firm for, for example, specialist tax or technology input when reviewing internal controls/risks – and they believe this enhances their ability to increase the value of the audit – which would be reduced if the audit practices were spun off into separate companies. This could act as the main rationale for the Big Four resisting pressure to split up.

In the last 5/10 years or so, each of the Big Four has set up their own Delivery Centres, often offshore and/or using less qualified personnel, to carry out the more routine and extensive procedures in a more cost effective way, albeit under the supervision of qualified auditors. However, this may be a transitionary position as the cost advantage is now being eroded, as for example India has resource limitations, and technology is rapidly advancing and should be able to take over much of this work.

If new technology assumes such a major part of the audit process, this begs the question in our minds whether or not technology firms (Google, Facebook, etc.) could become new entrants to the audit market, with them employing audit professionals in a supportive role to cover the judgmental aspects of an audit. This would certainly increase competition and add financially very strong participants.

In the medium term, this results in less competition and with the planned government move to increased PIEs audits, the position will worsen. The profession is becoming less attractive to young recruits but a broader role for auditors, for example, those involved in the ESG, and so on, aspects of the annual report, should increase the appeal.

The audit of riskier companies and audit orphans

Some major firms are unwilling to take on problem clients, for example, Sports Direct, due to the reputational risk and added to by the firms strong criticism of the retrospective and non-supportive attitude of the FRC.

The FT in an opinion piece noted 'The rising risk of "audit orphans" in a dysfunctional UK market'.[10] The FT also noted that the latest quality review by the FRC/ARGA highlights[11] a problem relating to the ambitious growth by mid-market firms such as Mazars and BDO. Overall, the share of inspected audits rated as good or requiring limited improvement rose for the third consecutive year. But the results at those two firms were dubbed 'unacceptable'. Both said they were investing to improve quality.

The FRC flagged another concern. The Big Four will continue to come under pressure to improve quality but in so doing they may jettison companies seen as higher-risk. This behaviour means problematic or complicated clients can end up with smaller firms, whose experience and systems may not really be up to the job. As a result, more companies could struggle to find an auditor, or ultimately be left orphaned by the market as has happened in other countries.[12]

As the FT article reported, the FRC sees mid-tier challenger firms as growing too fast and taking on the riskier audits that have been rejected by the Big Four:

> 'These firms have been growing too fast, picking up higher-risk audits being dropped by their peers, without adequate controls to ensure high-quality audits', the regulator said in its report.[13]

This leads to the Big Four cherry picking their audit clients whilst not tendering for the more risky audits. This leaves such audits to the smaller firms who perhaps have less resources and experience than the Big Four.

It is clear though that the Big Four, in safeguarding their reputations, have become more selective – a trend that is spreading to smaller firms, too. Auditors are starting to decline business not just where there are concerns around corporate governance or domineering management but where a sector with long-term contracts or heightened uncertainty means more subjective judgments that may be scrutinised unfavourably with hindsight. Another issue is where companies have significant chunks of business overseas, particularly in developing markets.[14]

Perhaps appointments to such clients could be supervised by a body such as the FRC/ARGA, helping to protect the appointed audit firm from reputational risk. Similarly, the riskiness of audit assignments can be reduced by having a more engaged audit committee. In this regard, it is interesting to see reports of more robust conversations between auditors and audit committees – encouraging better disclosure by the audit committee of problems and, thereby, obviating the need for adverse comment in the external audit report.

The mid-tier dichotomy

The lower PIE limit and increasing regulation by the FRC/ARGA creates a dichotomy of the small and mid-tier firms. The survival of the mid-tier firms is not their ability to undertake rigorous box-ticking and rigorous audits, but more to provide a general business service to the smaller business and to a much greater extent, add value to their clients. This is in stark contrast to the separation of audit and consultancy areas by the Big Four and some of the larger challenger firms. With these the split between audit and consultancy is becoming much more than just Chinese walls. EY took this to the logical extreme and planned to split the whole consultancy away as a separate company to provide EY with the growth they might achieve with the Big Tech companies and Silicon Valley businesses. This is where the job incentives are more enticing in tone.

We have discussed staff shortages and the difficulty of recruiting and then retaining professional staff by audit companies. That is made worse when you have an audit division suffering from reputational damage and with the staff possibly being censored and fined by the FRC/ARGA. This can encourage a potential two-way divide:

1 The Big Four and some of the larger challenger firms splitting off their audit divisions and concentrating on the 'box-ticking' type of audit that the FRC/ARGA increasingly regulates but hopefully reducing their exposure to fines and/or reprimands.
2 The smaller accounting firms become general business advisory firms providing a range of business services to help and support their clients.

Between these two end points, it is possible that mid-tier firms become caught in a bind. They are being encouraged to bid for new audit assignments in the hope that this stimulates the competitiveness of the audit market and brings enhancements in audit quality – yet, in the process, they will be under pressure to separate audit from their other services when, as firms, they probably provide the best quality of service to a corporate client when they are able to offer an all-round range of business services. Which probably means, strategically, that seeking to have a positive and progressive impact on corporate clients is something that such firms will be unlikely to pursue through audit – tendering for new, larger audit clients does not represent that attractive an option.

Could AI make a substantial difference to audit?

We hear much these days about the significance of artificial intelligence (AI). AI leverages computers and machines to mimic the problem-solving and decision-making capabilities of the human mind.

Artificial intelligence (AI) is the ability of a computer to do tasks that are usually done by humans because they require human intelligence and discernment. Usually the first AI systems struck success with games which are closed systems. Learning from repeated playing of games to some specified objective in order to learn the best moves – for example, checkmate in Chess.[15] Auditing is an open system. No two firms and at any particular time are ever identical.

Backwards propagation (historical data) is how those initial AI computer systems learnt. In machine learning, backpropagation is a widely used algorithm for training AI. For auditing, as no historical data is identical, auditors cannot be replaced by machines. Judgement also needs fine human discern. Auditing still needs the human touch. Right? No, absolutely not. Why? An order of magnitude leap in computing power. It is as if we were in the 18th century and trying to imagine space age travel. The change is quantum computing which is a next generation of computing technology that involves a type of computer at least 200 million times faster than the most sophisticated supercomputer we have in the world today. It is a device so powerful that it could do in nanoseconds what it would take a traditional supercomputer 10,000 years to accomplish. These are computers that can program other computers without human intervention.

These AI designed computers and their range of abilities are on par with human capabilities; or, probably, more capable than a human. More capable than a human with genetic modifications if that is ever allowed.

Facebook's parent company, Meta, is building the world's most powerful AI-specific supercomputer to develop better speech-recognition tools, automatically translate between different languages and help build its 3D virtual metaverse.[16] When this computer, called the RSC (Research Super Cluster) is complete, it will consist of more than 20,000 GPUs (each processor being tailored to AI learning and costing upwards of $200,000 each).

Meta claims that at this point, it will be the fastest AI-optimised supercomputer in the world, performing at more than 5 exaflops. An exaflop computer system is capable of performing one quintillion floating-point operations per second. Quantum computers will be several orders of magnitude faster than that.

Meta's machine is specialised to train and run large AI models. There will be more powerful computers in the world when it is complete, but only a few, and none that share its exact architecture or intended use. The cutting edge of AI research has relied on scale in recent years, and ever more powerful machines to train models with. One of the largest neural networks, the Megatron-Turing Natural Language Generation model, has 530 billion parameters, which are roughly equivalent to the connections between brain cells. Meta says its machine will eventually run models with trillions of parameters. The Meta computer will be billed as a slow old generation computer once quantum computing matures. That is the order of magnitude we need to make auditing AI systems.

Ok so what has this got to do with auditing? Well once we get to the situation where one super quantum computer can program another quantum computer all bets are off. We get back to the situation where an AI computer can be more capable than a professional trained auditor with experience. How you might ask?

So one computer can program another and also create vast amounts of synthetic data for AI training another computer – all in a nano-second or faster with trillions of scenarios backwards and forward in time (i.e. simulations of every possible human interactions and every possible transaction). All in a blink of an eyelid. Containment of such technology is just not possible. That combined with the shortage of accounting and auditing staff will hasten the takeover of these AI trained quantum computer systems. We were sceptical but the creation of synthetic history and futures to train AI computers in a fraction of a second changes all that.

Redefining audit and assurance for an AI world

AI creating synthetic data to enable other AI computers to undertake audits. That is in the passive historical role. What is fascinating though is that the synthetic data can be forward in time simulations and hence teach the AI audit computer how to help companies do better in a future proactive role. Of course that leaves open what we might define as better. And whatever we define as better may be redefined by the AI computers: the AI teacher (and creator of synthetic data) and the AI audit learner computer. Of course it is wrong to talk about a computer – these will be networks of computers. .

Between them they may redefine audit and enable an entirely new and positive role for audit. Education? Leave that to the AI computers?

AI is no immediate answer

Of course, this scenario is some distance away in time. Meanwhile the role of auditors is expanding and the shortage of personnel (especially qualified staff) will continue. One answer to the shortage is to go further than just an administrative split between audit and consultancy divisions.

EY's attempted solution

EY's global proposal, featuring a break-up of the Big Four firm, was claimed to have its consulting division with an opportunity to generate up to $10 billion in extra fees by liberating it from conflicts of interest that block partnerships with the world's largest tech groups.[17] EY dominates the auditing of large US tech companies, including the accounts of Amazon, Google, Oracle, Salesforce and Workday. In an interview with the Financial Times, EY's CEO, Carmine Di Sibio, described his firm's position in the tech audit market as both a blessing and a curse. The same FT article[18] reported:

> While its strength was positive for the audit business, Di Sibio said this was also a 'negative' because it meant EY was prevented by conflict of interest rules from entering alliances to work alongside some of the world's biggest technology companies on projects for their other clients.
>
> These tie-ups between professional services and tech groups are key to winning lucrative consulting contracts to help corporate clients with projects such as upgrading IT systems for

managing supply chains and other operations so they can run in the cloud.

When EY committed to keeping both its audit and advisory operations almost a decade ago, it had not anticipated how important cloud technology and partnerships with tech companies would become, said Di Sibio.

Over time, the standalone advisory business would win between $5bn and $10bn a year in consulting fees that are currently 'off the table' because conflicts rules restrict it from working alongside the likes of Amazon or Salesforce, he added.

Independence from the consulting arm would allow the audit business to bid for more mandates and to expand more quickly by rebuilding its advisory operations, Di Sibio said.

EY's decision not to go ahead with a split, which would have been judged by some as the biggest shake-up of the auditing and accounting industry in two decades, could have reshaped the industry and been one possibility to overcome staff shortages. Join the tech firms. But then EY would also have had to start paying tech salaries but presumably EY thought it would have been worth it.

Meanwhile the other three of the Big Four are unlikely to pursue a historic split and so the main EY competitors continue to stand by their model of offering audit and consulting, albeit through separate divisions that will not ease the staff shortages and the capacity constraints.

New entrants

It is surprising that there have been no new entrants in to the field of auditing. Low profit margins and the problems of auditing risky businesses with potential fines and sanctions offer a barrier to new entrants. We are not surprised to see talk of audit fees increasing but this is not a sufficient answer to the problems facing audit. A longer-term solution has to embrace a fundamental re-think of audit in ways that enhance the added value it provides.

New emphasis on digital and technology jobs

Meanwhile back in the real world there is a new emphasis on digital and technology jobs. The FT notes a KPMG development[19] is investing £5.5m in its flagship One St Peter's Square offices in Manchester, leading to new digital and technology jobs as part of the investment. KPMG will build Ignition North, a new 25,000 square feet collaborative hub designed to spark innovation and support digital transformation, as well as redesigning its wider office space.

We believe that other firms, especially PwC and RSM, also have specific projects geared to digital and IT work and training. In fact most firms are moving in this direction. Digital is impossible to ignore and just about everything a PIE company will do is digitised and computerised. This highlights the developing changes in how staff are trained and recruited as well as office tech hubs for both staff and clients.

Notes

1 www.curtisrecruitment.co.uk/accountants-short-numbers/
2 One GP known to one of the authors is earning over £250,000 and takes up to 2 months holidays a year – to stay at his overseas properties.
3 www.theguardian.com/business/2022/jul/07/pwc-partners-to-earn-1m-each-as-firm-sets-new-pay-records
4 www.accountancyage.com/2022/06/09/qa-mazars-on-dissecting-the-uks-draft-audit-reform-bill/
5 www.accountancyage.com/2022/06/09/qa-mazars-on-dissecting-the-uks-draft-audit-reform-bill/
6 www.ft.com/content/f9f21521-f354-42ed-92d3-ee9cf68e1534
7 www.accountancyage.com/2022/06/09/qa-mazars-on-dissecting-the-uks-draft-audit-reform-bill/
8 www.accountancyage.com/2022/06/09/qa-mazars-on-dissecting-the-uks-draft-audit-reform-bill/
9 Overall, I do see it as positive benefit to the economy. The government has listened, and it hasn't gone over the top in regulation. I think their positioning on UK SOX is partly driven by that, because that would have created significant additional compliance work for businesses and boards. Once the bill is through, and we've got clarity and certainty, we're probably going to be in a stronger position as an ecosystem which should be attractive to investors.
10 www.ft.com/content/b70244b3-2585-49a0-beb4-973fb9faef47
11 www.frc.org.uk/news/july-2022/frc-publishes-latest-audit-quality-review-results
12 www.ft.com/content/b70244b3-2585-49a0-beb4-973fb9faef47

13 www.thetimes.co.uk/article/challenger-audit-firms-on-back-foot-as-big-four-drop-riskier-clients-snj06hntz

14 www.ft.com/content/b70244b3-2585-49a0-beb4-973fb9faef47

15 Krish Bhaskar was lucky enough to be involved in what would become a world beating chess program (Chess 4.0) at the first signs of crud artificial intelligence in the late 1960s on CDC 7600 then supercomputers.

16 www.newscientist.com/article/2305606-meta-is-building-the-worlds-largest-ai-specific-supercomputer/#:~:text=Facebook's%20parent%20company%2C%20Meta%2C%20is,build%20its%203D%20virtual%20metaverse.
www.newscientist.com/article/2305606-meta-is-building-the-worlds-largest-ai-specific-supercomputer/

17 www.ft.com/content/4b544040-8cf1-454a-823f-63077f068a42

18 www.ft.com/content/4b544040-8cf1-454a-823f-63077f068a42

19 www.thebusinessdesk.com/northwest/news/2106675-kpmg-investing-5.5m-in-manchester-office-creating-digital-and-tech-jobs

4 Regulation and the audit market

The importance of culture

When a good one third of the US population can believe the 2020 election was stolen, and a sizeable proportion of that sane body believes in the ex-President's continued lies, then we can see classic traits of inflated ego, attention seeking, few empathies and fewer boundaries. The same may be said of many of the large failures – such as Wirecard and may be Patisserie Valerie closer to home. Some might say that Sir Philip Green and Sanjeev Gupta fit the same mould. What is clear is that the regulations promulgated by ARGA/FRC are not enough. There has to be more – more of an examination of the culture of the company. Elon Musk tried to adopt an entirely different managerial style at Twitter and it nearly cost him the company. That said Sam Bankman-Fried ran FTX as a 'personal fiefdom' according to the court papers as reported by the BBC.[1]

So regulations are not enough. Is it a necessary and sufficient condition for audit quality? The culture of an organisations, we argue is just as important and there is no manual of auditing that can pronounce or deduce this without humans picking up the scent of such a culture.

FRC

Having poured through all the FRC publications over time and tried, often in vain, to make sense of the numbers and figures in their report, we have come to the conclusion that the FRC is still failing to be transparent.

DOI: 10.4324/9780429273865-4

Despite this, much more resource is being poured into the FRC with a doubling of its headcount and establishing a second office in Birmingham as it is outgrowing its London Wall base. The government paper did not change in any way the functions of the proposed transition to ARGA. In fact, it may seem to hand more control (and therefore size) to ARGA as it would need to adjudicate a much more woolly set of government guidelines that are not strictly enshrined in law.

The FRC has ramped up its regulatory stance since 2018 with a wide range of initial (and full) investigations and enquiries, many of which result in sanctions and fines. The latter, whilst allowing for a discount for cooperation and early settlement, have increased notably.

Our analysis is that there are currently announced or past cases reported publicly 107 cases and allowing for some duplication 86 unique cases. The total fines levied including costs awarded are £178 million and a further estimated £68m (perhaps as large as £100m) to come from the publicly announced cases. This has involved 67 audit partners (including 6 juniors) and 37 accountants in business.

The level of fines are likely to increase rising to over £10m per case and we expect the number of directors in business sanctioned to exponentially increase with the new 2022 regulations – when enacted.

The largest fines were:

a The £14.4m fines by KPMG in 2022 for providing misleading or false documents or representations (Carillion and Regeneris). That still leaves a possible fine for errors in the Carillion audits. With costs this came to £18.7m so far.
b The largest fine to date was issued to Deloitte in £15m in 2020 for the audits of Autonomy before its sale to HP in 2011. (That case took a long time to resolve). With costs that case rose to £20.6m.
c The KPMG audit of Silentnight where the fine was £13m excluding costs.

To date the Big Four in confidential interviews treat these fines as just a cost of doing business. All the fines relate to the same issue as the root cause – insufficient scepticism and/or lack of adequate audit evidence.

The Big Four or Group of 30 plus auditors are under the FRC scrutiny and this is becoming an ever-increasing list as the FRC amplifies its scrutiny to all PIE audits – even though the definition of public interest is a sore point with the smaller firms under scrutiny.

There does not seem to be any significant reputational damage. Quite the reverse. The scope and extent of audits are increasing and the shortage of staff makes these larger firms picky and exacting about their criteria for tendering or undertaking an audit.

Resilience of the audit market

The bigger question is not whether fines will affect the auditors but whether the possibility of legal action might result in financial hardship and possible failure or merger of the larger auditing firms. For example:

- KPMG has being sued for £1.3 billion by the liquidators of Carillion, who claim the auditor missed signs that the firm's accounts were misstated and that the group was insolvent more than two years before it collapsed.[2]
- KPMG settled its case with Quindell (now called Watchstone) for £5m.[3]
- EY was being sued for at least $2.5 billion for alleged negligence in its audits of NMC Health, the health group that collapsed in a suspected multibillion-dollar fraud.[4]
- PwC has been sued by administrators of racing car dealership JD Classics over allegations the Big Four firm negligently failed to spot fraud, causing losses of more than £41m.[5]
- EY also has a UK case (Rihan v EY) dealing with a whistleblowing matter which lawyers and analysts believe will have major ramifications for the auditing industry.[6] This involved the audit of a Dubai gold refining company.

Internationally, these cases continued to escalate:

- PwC were being sued in a New Zealand court for allegedly providing wrong advice to companies in the Brierley group,[7]

- In Australia a professional negligence suit against PwC, by failed education provider Cornerstone was dismissed, but the collapsed firm will be allowed to file an improved claim as legal actions against the major accounting firms continue to mount up.
- PwC also settled a case in Australia over its allegedly deficient work for media company Broadcast Operations.
- EY and Pitcher Partners were in a case over their audits of law firm Slater & Gordon before its near collapse in 2015.
- Deloitte was being sued over the audit of a failed oil trader in Singapore that owes creditors more than $3.5 billion. This suit alleges Deloitte failed to detect irregularities in the financial statements of Hin Leong Trading Ltd. for more than a decade.[8]
- KPMG was also in a court case in Australia over its audits CuDeco's financial reports that were 'materially misleading' and 'not based upon reasonable grounds'.[9]
- KPMG also faced a shareholder class action in the Victorian Supreme Court over its audit work for collapsed steel maker Arrium.[10]
- KPMG was also being sued over its role in the insolvency of Dubai private equity firm Abraaj Group.[11]

It might be argued that the UK is becoming more conscious of legal cases against auditors. Some believe that the legal impact of auditors failing to raise the red flags of potential insolvencies are increasing.[12]

Given the pandemic and the resulting supply problems, couple that with the war in Ukraine and sanctions against Russia, the opportunities for possible insolvencies will increase. That may mean bigger and possibly bitter lawsuits.

Press comments are proving to be more in favour of auditor liability.[13] A study[14] by Lennox and Li, found that auditors are more likely to be included as co-defendants when the accounting allegations involve fictitious assets and/or reductions of expenses. For example, an overstatement of inventory on the balance sheet and an understatement of cost of goods sold on the income statement. Auditors are also more likely to be sued when the allegations include overvalued assets or undervalued liabilities and expenses.[15]

Reputational damage

The total fines and cost of the FRC's cases against the Big Four as of June 2022 were:

	No of cases	*Fines and costs so far as end 2022*
Deloitte	11	£38m
EY	4	£7m
KPMG	16	£76m
BDO	2	N/A
GT	11	£16m*
Mazars	3	£2m*

These figures may be disputed as the FRC does not always reveal the total fines and costs. Some cases may not be revealed. The bottom line is that KPMG has probably been involved in more noteworthy cases starting from before Carillion onwards. KPMG has also had by far the largest fines.

GT and Mazars have several outstanding cases, but they level of fines imposed on their respective firms may have a much greater impact than that for the Big Four (www.accountingweb.co.uk/community/blogs/richardmurphy/how-long-can-kpmg-last).

Notes

1 www.bbc.co.uk/news/business-63720310
2 www.ft.com/content/94c89c70-f8fb-4867-a283-4a8a151060ad
3 www.ft.com/content/d677b67f-e2f0-49f4-a753-786fe05d4c7c
4 www.ft.com/content/4314e1e2-3418-48b9-bd86-49f1c2c1a7ce
5 www.ft.com/content/baed7799-a314-468c-ad8b-88ca590b2af1 See also www.seddons.co.uk/our-thinking/final-notice-audit-legal-impact-auditors-failing-raise-red-flags-potential
6 www.law.com/international-edition/2020/08/20/rihan-v-ey-the-case-that-shook-the-big-four-and-beyond/?slreturn=20220508104155
7 www.stuff.co.nz/business/industries/125617853/pwc-sued-for-15b-for-allegedly-providing-wrong-advice-to-brierley-companies
8 www.insurancejournal.com/news/international/2021/06/10/618225.htm
9 www.afr.com/companies/professional-services/kpmg-sued-over-audit-work-for-collapsed-miner-20220426-p5ag57

10 www.afr.com/companies/professional-services/kpmg-sued-over-audit-work-for-collapsed-miner-20220426-p5ag57

11 www.straitstimes.com/business/banking/kpmg-sued-for-814-million-over-alleged-sloppy-auditing-in-dubais-abraaj-scandal

12 www.seddons.co.uk/our-thinking/final-notice-audit-legal-impact-auditors-failing-raise-red-flags-potential

13 www.bloomberg.com/news/articles/2021-08-05/auditors-coming-under-increased-scrutiny-from-london-courts

14 https://papers.ssrn.com/sol3/papers.cfm?abstract_id=3480706

15 www.forbes.com/sites/josephbrazel/2020/09/08/when-are-audit-firms-sued-for-financial-reporting-failures/?sh=1dc2b8e2e301

5 The Groundhog Day merry-go-round or a new audit concept

The timeline – reform follows financial failures and scandals

In the quest for examining the possibilities to the answer to the book's quest of 'Audit and Regulatory Reform – Implications for the Profession' and in particular the specific question of 'How do we make auditing a positive and progressive force for good?' we highlight a conundrum. Consider these corporate failures and then the corresponding tightening of regulations, including auditing standards and rules.

The scandal	*The result*
1929 Wall Street Crash	1933 Securities Act (US)[1]
1938 McKesson & Robbins[2]	Professional auditing standards developed.
	SEC adoption of conservative accounting rules, including a 30-year ban on upward asset valuations
	In the UK the ICAEW's 29 non-mandatory improvements in financial reporting practices issued between 1942 and 1969 tended to promote conservatism.
1970 Penn Central[3] among	The SEC established the Financial Accounting

DOI: 10.4324/9780429273865-5

The scandal	*The result*
Others	Standards Board and other regulations.
1990 Polly Peck[4] and others[5]	Reform and moves to improve accounting standards and corporate governance. The newly formed Accounting Standards Board revised accounting practice highlighted as deficient in the Polly Peck case, including cash flow statements, off-balance sheet finance and foreign currency translation.
2001 Enron[6] among others	The failure of Arthur Andersen[7] and the resulting Sarbanes-Oxley Act (US)[8]
2007–09 Global Financial Crisis	Including the failure of Lehman Brothers[9] and the Royal Bank Scotland/NatWest[10] (RBS) rescue by the UK government. This led to the tightening of rules right across the EU including multiple changes to company law and the creation of PIEs and the FRC in 2012 among other regulatory bodies and regulations.
2017 Carillion collapse	Augmented by Patisserie Valerie[11] in 2018 and Wirecard[12] in 2020 in Germany. Carillion was probably the trigger for the various reviews, reports, suggested tightening of the regulations in the UK despite Brexit.
	Other cases range from BHS to P&O Ferries. One issue creating a number of financial issues was Greensill, and the Sanjeev Gupta Empire.

The one single issue that is shown is the fact that reform follows financial failures and scandals. Current critiques would claim that no director of a publicly-listed company has ever been imprisoned for failing to spot fraud in their business, though the some of the directors' of Carillion have been fined £870,000.[13]

It seems that it is always the auditors that are blamed for the major part of financial failures that arise from the failure of corporate management.

> Auditor reports specifically tell investors that financial statements are the responsibility of management and that the role of the auditor is to give an opinion as to whether they are true and fair. This opinion is based on the relevant accounting standards, using accepted auditing practices. These practices are designed to reduce the risk of error and fraud to a suitably low level – they are not designed to eliminate risk.
>
> Post-failure investigation is important: it is not acceptable for auditors to fall short of professional standards. But neither should we rush to judgement that a business failure, a financial misstatement or even a fraud is necessarily an auditor failure.[14]

With hindsight, actions could have been better. KPMG has paid the price:

> KPMG is set to be hit with its biggest-ever fine in the UK after a tribunal found that its auditors deliberately misled regulators during routine inspections of its work.

The fine was reduced to £14.4 million and 4 individuals excluded with their careers more or less ruined. A junior was reprimanded but not required to pay a fine on review.[15]

Jon Holt, UK chief executive of KPMG, said the misconduct was 'unjustifiable and wrong'. It was right that the firm and its former auditors should face 'serious regulatory sanctions', he said. 'We have worked hard, and with complete transparency to our regulator, to assure ourselves that this matter does not represent the wider culture or practice of our firm', he added.

The tribunal was not asked to assess whether KPMG's audits of Carillion or Regenersis were substantively flawed, only whether its auditors had misled the FRC during routine regulatory inspections of its work. The FRC is running separate investigations into possible failings in the Carillion audits. KPMG, which has been fined more than £34mn for misconduct in the UK in the past four years, has said it will defend a £1.3bn negligence claim against it by Carillion's liquidators. The government has also launched legal action seeking to ban eight former directors of Carillion from UK boardrooms. (See updates in Chapter 10).

Audit in disrepute

The KPMG fines emanating from 2016 and the subsequent cover-up, and the original audit work on Carillion has placed its staff and partners in a difficult position. The cover-up[16] involved the auditors misleading the FRC, by creating documents during an inspection that were then presented to the watchdog as if they had been produced before Carillion's 2016 accounts were signed off. KPMG did admit to the cover-up.[17] KPMG agreed to pay the fine of £20 million for its misconduct (reduced to £14.4 million) and £4.3 million in costs. Many of KPMG's staff were also fined smaller amounts. This fine was the second-largest ever handed to a UK accounting firm, eclipsed only by the £15 million penalty imposed on Deloitte in 2020 for its auditing failures at Autonomy (discussed in Book 1[18]).

However, these staff fines have led to some hardship for junior colleagues – who might say they were just following orders from their seniors.[19] That same FT report identified the misery and ruination of a junior's career with the added issue that any fine might lead the person to financial failure.

All this occurred whilst we were writing the book. We have been thinking hard about this latest set of news items. At one level, it feels like it serves to set back any calls for less regulation as the breaches/cases inevitably stir things up even more and demand more things to be introduced to constrain or improve what auditors do. But at another level they really also should serve to question what is going on? Do we really know enough, not only as to why these things happen but what is the ruling culture and working arrangements in audit? PwC, like many other firms, has a whole commitment to developing a culture of challenge in audit and KPMG has tried to change its culture: 'KPMG's partners in the UK have been told they risk forfeiting their share of the £300 million proceeds retained from the sales of its pensions and insolvency divisions if they fail to meet ethical standards'.[20] That said, we still know relatively little about the way in which firms are run (e.g. whether or not audit is profitable), the internal standing of, and impacts on, the day-to-day realities of audit work (despite frequent stories in the press regarding claims of excessive working hours and mandatory (not 'voluntary') overtime without pay abound).[21]

While press coverage can be illuminating it can also be a source of confusion. Some newspaper reports lack depth and can be driven by a desire to 'dramatise', if not 'scandalise'. Analysis of remedies and solutions can result in more questions than answers – with frequent switches in sentiment from claims that there is too much regulation to complaints when regulations are dropped. Even supposedly serious broadsheet newspapers can at times appear somewhat caricatural in their representation of audit – although there are some examples where detailed investigative reporting have broken major cases of audit failure (such as the Financial Times' pursuit of the Wirecard scandal).

We almost get to the stage where it feels like the reporting and the various investigations of and responses to scandals serve to prevent serious discussion of conceptual change and does encourage old hobby horses to be raised again and again. Then again looking at this from the auditing staff viewpoint, we would like to see more of KPMG from the inside and for people to explain frankly and seriously what has been going on. It is not one dimensional. But the legal/investigative environment probably will never enable this as people are essentially looking to protect their backs and promote their own significance. We hear a lot about the importance of holistic thinking and everyone agrees with it. But do we get much of it in these repeating situations – the Groundhog Day scenario. Or is it that everyone's holistic thinking differs in terms of focus and remedy?

Conceptually, it also is worth considering what the inspection and cultural context in firms is doing to how audit and audit quality is represented. Much seems to be about getting robust documentation, to such a degree that data reconstruction or fabrication occurs.

Groundhog Day for audit

So, as outlined above, there is a very lengthy history of financial crises and scandals. In every case the response is that the problem is not necessarily an event attributed to the external financial audit but a wider problem of management performance, financial reporting and governance. As Humphrey et al. (1993) commented:[22]

> There will be a gigantic fraud. The auditors will fail to detect it, and will be surprised when they read about it, at the same time as everybody else, in the pages of *The Sunday Times*. The profession will be heavily criticised. The auditing guideline on fraud will be reviewed ... There will be nothing new under the sun.[23]

So this is sometimes described as Groundhog Day after the film where Phil Connors (acted by Bill Murray), plays a cynical television weatherman covering the annual Groundhog Day event in the US who becomes trapped in a time loop, forcing him to relive that day repeatedly.

Corporate responsibility and audit

Audit is one element in a complex chain of corporate responsibility and governance. We have already commented that the FRC has taken action against auditors whereas almost no action is taken against the directors and management of the company charged with misleading information and/or fraud. Instead, emphasis tends to concentrate on strengthening the regulation and market conditions associated with the existing form of audit instead of reforming other aspects of corporate reporting and governance.

Discussions often centre around the auditor's responsibility with respect to the detection of company fraud and other illegal acts. In this instance the auditor becomes a 'bloodhound or a watchdog', but what is the auditor's capacity to apply something that is more intrusive and akin to forensic auditing.

We question the degree of reliance that can be placed upon an auditor's opinion, the length of which has been increasing over time, by the financial world and the public, especially in terms of the level of assurance that an audited entity is a going concern and is viable. 'Going concern' examines the survivability of the company over the next 12 months. 'Viability' looks forward several years.

The trouble when corporate failures and scandals occur is that the same set of questions are always asked:

- Were the auditors too trusting of management?
- Did the auditors show sufficient scepticism?

Beasley (2001)[24] listed 5 issues that led to audit deficiencies in a US study:

1 Auditors could learn to better detect fraud through learning from mistakes
2 The auditors failure to gather sufficient audit evidence.
3 The auditors failed to follow accounting standards or applied them incorrectly.
4 Auditors failed to properly assess inherent risk and adjust the audit program accordingly.
5 Failure to exercise due professional care and the appropriate level of professional scepticism.

Conway[25] goes on to claim that his experiences of working inside the profession and as a regulator in the US was that the auditing firms competed primarily on cost. His recommendations were that auditors should provide a range of metrics such as:

- The average years of experience of the audit professionals
- Ratio of professional staff to audit partners including an allowance for outsourcing
- Chargeable hours per audit professional
- Professional chargeable hours per audit partner
- Annual professional staff retention
- Average annual training hours per professional

Conway also blamed:[26]

> The fundamental risk of this business model is that audits conducted by inexperienced staff with minimal year-over-year

> continuity pose a heightened risk of undetected errors leading to an audit failure. This heightened risk is compounded by the concurrent risk that the audit may not adequately supervised due to heavy partner and manager workloads. Further compounding this risk is the perception that reporting deadlines are seemingly fixed, leaving some auditors wishing they had more time to conduct a better audit. This business model is a complete mismatch for the complexity auditors need to master in today's environment to achieve suitable levels of audit quality.

The reporting ecosystem

Deloitte's put this as follows:

> The financial reporting ecosystem is necessarily irreducible – meaning that each part is integral to the proper functioning of the others – and, therefore, the entire ecosystem must adapt in concert and with speed. Management, audit committees, regulators, policy-makers, standard-setters, investors and auditors are in this together! It's important to remember that the purpose of the financial reporting ecosystem is to serve the public interest by enabling complete, accurate, transparent corporate financial disclosures.[27]

Each constituent part is dependent on each other. Audit is a significant part of this system. Change anything in this system and it will probably impact on audit and auditing. Although the term 'ecosystem' initially came into existence around ESG affairs, it is now commonly referring to the system as described above. Each component has an effect on the others – if one changes this will ripple through all the other components – audit included.

> Historically, the dominant tendency has been to accept that audit is a secondary function, whose value fundamentally depends on the value of the financial reports whose truth and fairness is being assured by auditors. Improve financial reporting, develop financial reporting standards (and any underlying conceptual framework) or enhance other elements or processes of corporate governance, and the value and effectiveness of audit will, in turn, be enhanced.[28]

The rapid development of ecosystems is presenting financial service providers with major operational and strategic challenges. A survey of Swiss and German financial service providers focused in particular on the current and future positioning of the financial industry in ecosystems, the use of digital platforms for the exchange of data, the necessary expertise of employees, corporate culture and regulation.

Ecosystems in the financial services industry

Ecosystems in the context of the survey are dynamically evolving communities of businesses, consumers and institutions that share resources in a common market (e.g. through a platform), adding value in a common business model.

For financial service providers, a question arises as to whether and how they want to position themselves in newly-emerging ecosystems, and how they want to structure their products and services. Participation in ecosystems offers them considerable benefits, including greater customer retention and focus, new forms of revenue generation, integration with specialised partners and sharing of costs. However, significant risks must also be taken into account, such as loss of customer interfaces, data security concerns, reduced margins, loss of control and loss of brand identity.

The audit ecosystem

Financial reports and corporate reports have that final stamp of ‘approval’ in the audit report and the opinion contained therein. Audit is, perhaps wrongly, regarded as providing verification and/or assurance on corporate and financial reports. That gives rise to the concept of audits and financial markets as being ‘linked ecologies’ in some way. The common notion is that it is not the audit ecosystem but a financial reporting ecosystem.

The audit ecosystem has been mentioned for some time. You Tube has Vasarhelyi[29] lecturing us on The Audit Ecosystem in a somewhat techno view of auditing. It is however more general and involves intelligent agents among cloud-based systems, and other IT-based concepts. Earlier, Fornelli[30] presented a paper to the Centre for Audit Quality[31] and argued for strengthening the ecosystem for audit quality. The paper stressed the importance of restatements of public company financial statements.

> Indeed, we think that preparers, auditors and investors benefit greatly from being well-informed on the types of financial restatements, the accounting issues that resulted in the need for a restatement, and the severity of those issues.

From this we can see that this paper primarily focused on financial reporting and investors. Not so much about auditing *per se*.

Kozlowski in Continuous Auditing[32] couched the audit ecosystem as a complete accounting and assurance system based on blockchains. This is framed as one particular adaptation of accounting systems and follows a long line of new accounting systems.[33] Also that might need reconsideration in the light that blockchains are not quite as safe as originally envisaged. Numerous examples are given.[34] Recent examples citing fraud abound[35] with much money lost[36] and the take-up of blockchains has not been as great as techno wizards had warned, in part because blockchains are just ledgers with a little more sophisticated encryption and a degree of anonymity (but not necessarily absolute).

The International Federation of Accountants (IFAC),[37] makes reference to an audit and assurance ecosystem. IFAC mentions the importance of having the 'right' audit that meets stakeholder expectations and in the audit and assurance eco-system acting to improve the audit process:

> Achieving high-quality audits requires a well-functioning ecosystem built upon ethics and independence, preconditions to achieving high-quality audits. This ecosystem involves a number of factors and participants including the right people, the right governance, and the right regulation. These elements must all work together to produce the right audit that meets the expectations of stakeholders. The quality of audit must be assessed by the right measurements. In the absence of any of these components, the audit may not meet the expectations of stakeholders.[38]
>
> All participants in the audit and assurance ecosystem must act to improve the audit process, the skill-set and mind-set

> of accounting professionals, the governance activities of companies and firms, the regulations and standards that support entity reporting and auditor behaviour, and how audit quality is assessed.

More recently the ACCA reinforced the concept of auditing within the corporate reporting ecosystem:[39]

> Reform reviews, both in the EU and globally, are currently proposing radical changes of the wider financial reporting ecosystem. These reforms relate to the three main pillars – namely audit, corporate governance and the supervision and enforcement of these (as identified by the European Commission in the EU) – contributing to high-quality and reliable corporate reporting.

Relationship between audit and assurance

Audit and the audit ecosystem can be redefined in terms of a new thematic view. Humphrey et al. (2021; 2024) highlighted that the possibilities for audit development and conceptual reframing are immediately made much more substantial if the presumed relationship between audit and assurance is reversed. Thus, rather than audit being a subset of a broader range of assurance services, assurance becomes a subset of audit (i.e. assurance is just one potential form of audit service and audit is freed from just being centred around lending assurance to reported information). Could it be possible, for example, for audit to satisfy accountability demands and serve the public interest through independent investigative means that directly enable the company to perform and to be better?

What becomes critical here is both the definition of audit and that of an eco-system. The above traditional depictions typically adopt a very singular view of audit and if there is any representation of an audit eco-system it is very much one of a support network designed to assist and enable the provision of one, given, form of 'audit' in a 'quality' manner. However, as Humphrey et al. (2024) argued, it is possible to view things in different and more expansive ways. In the Brydon report, 'the purpose of an audit is to help establish and maintain deserved confidence in a company, in its directors and in the information for which they have responsibility to report, including the financial statements'.

> This opens up the possibility of envisaging a quite different representation of an audit ecosystem – one that that is not centred on the delivery and support of a singular, defined form of audit. Natural ecosystems are typically referred to as dynamic communities of living organisms interacting with each other in a given area and with their non-living environment.

While the word 'ecosystem' was almost unused in the financial services world a few years ago, today it is on the top of the agenda of every bank and insurance company. As always, with such a loaded term, it is important to take first a step back and oversee the bigger picture.

Audit – what can we agree upon?

What can accountants and auditors agree to in general. Some may feel that the audit ecosystem is a concept too far. Some may still prefer to view audit as a subset of assurance. Some may regard audit as being always the final stamp of approval in corporate reports, and/or the watchdog certifying that nothing has gone amiss in the entity being audited.

With delays over the development of ARGA, this invites a renewed interest and speculation about the RSBs. In particular, such bodies could become more of a driving force in terms of regulatory developments as illustrated by the ICAEW's recent challenge to the FRC proposed revisions to the audit firm governance code:

> ICAEW believes the 2022 proposed revisions to the Code lack clarity, are excessively prescriptive and extend beyond the original purpose of the Code. It urges the FRC to address these concerns and present any changes within a compelling, cohesive package that enhances audit committee and investor engagement.[40]

We can agree that audit is in part a social function, involving many more elements than simply the corporation and its shareholders. Just seeing relevant stakeholders as being the shareholders or the investment community is too narrow. In an ideal world, the scope of audit should be expanded, notably to cover governance and sustainability. If a corporation's management had manipulated the election system in a way that the current management was always re-elected, shareholders, the public and the government would all like to know about it, and the obvious person to inform them is the auditor. The same consideration applies when the corporation is causing large quantities of green-house-gases to be emitted into the atmosphere (with the global net-zero initiative).

So, where does audit and assurance have to go or develop? Can it be more than a policing role? Can it become a service that might help the entity being audited and, thereby, be more of a direct benefit to a broad range of stakeholders?

We believe that the audit currently places far too much emphasis on the financial statements. There is a host of research that indicates that the financial statements are becoming increasing unimportant as a source of information about a corporation's activities.[41]

Widening the scope of audit

The limited scope of current auditing is a principal reason why many commentators dismiss audit as a factor in solving society's problems (see British Academy report, page 14[42]). The core of the problem is that reporting should not be limited to the financial statements; the term 'financial reporting' should be replaced by 'corporate reporting' to reflect that a host of other matters should be covered, including governance, sustainability, ESG and so on.

What we might propose are two fundamentally different concepts of audit: the proactive audit and the passive audit:[43]

- In a 'proactive' audit, the auditor seeks to improve the performance of the audited entity.
- In a 'passive' audit, the auditor makes no attempt to change the entity's actions; he restricts his function to reporting on them.

The distinction can be made clearer by considering current practice. The term 'audit' in Wikipedia,[44] shows many examples of activities that would be classified as proactive audits; two are particularly pertinent:

1 Energy audit: The auditor investigates how the entity (which can be anything from a household to a giant corporation) uses energy and makes recommendations as to how it may use energy more efficiently.
2 Clinical audit. This is a procedure that has been introduced into public health systems of many countries, including the UK's NHS. It has been defined as 'a quality improvement process that seeks to improve patient care and outcomes through systematic review of care against explicit criteria'.

We believe that this last sentence is particularly relevant. An essential feature of a proactive audit is that the criteria against which the entity's performance is judged are clearly defined. Commonly, the auditor can define the criteria, and, in all cases, accepts them as appropriate. Frequently the auditor has access to the entity's inner workings (either because the entity's management acknowledges the utility of the audit, or because a body with authority over the entity so decides). But this is not an invariable feature of a proactive audit; for example, an NGO can undertake a social audit of a corporation without access to the corporation's systems, using such information that is publicly available.

The standard example in the UK of a passive audit is the audit of a corporation's financial statements. The criteria that govern the audit are not set by the auditor; they are set by the law; the Companies Act states that the auditor should report on whether the financial statements give 'a true and fair view' and the Courts of Law have interpreted this term as requiring that the financial statements be drawn up in conformity with applicable accounting standards. The auditor plays no active role in either the management of the corporation or (in theory) in the preparation of the financial statement.

The normal fundamental principle is that the auditor should not report on his or her own work, for this would constitute an unacceptable conflict of interest. The value of a passive audit is that, if well done, it increases the confidence of people outside the corporation in the competence and integrity of the corporation's management. These outsiders, whose principal source of information about the corporation's activities is the information supplied by the management, are naturally sceptical that management will report fully and truthfully about its own performance. With the passive audit, the auditor reports on another's work; the value of the audit lies in increased confidence and trust.

With the proactive audit, the value of the audit resides in the work performed by the auditor. It would seem that the term 'audit' can refer to two fundamentally different activities: the proactive audit aims to create value (or at least help to avoid a reduction in value), through the entity's improved performance; the passive audit aims to increase trust.

What do these two activities have in common? We believe that they have much in common, notably:

- Expertise; Both types of audit are undertaken by skilled professionals, who provide an expertise not present in the entity's own workforce.
- Independence: With both types of audit, the value is enhanced by the auditor being independent of the entity. With the passive audit, the auditor must be completely independent of the management, for otherwise the outsiders to whom the auditor reports, will suspect that the report simply presents the management's viewpoint. With the proactive audit, an outside auditor can bring a fresh perspective to the investigation of the entity's activities, perhaps one that the entity's staff have not previously considered, out of deference to the management.
- Integrity: With both types of audit, the value of the audit depends crucially on the auditor being scrupulously honest in his work.

These communalities imply that it will often be appropriate and efficient, for both types of audit to be undertaken by the same person, such as a skilled and experienced professional. But it should be acknowledged that they are fundamentally different activities. In particular, any attempt to expand the scope of the current financial audit of the corporation to cover matters that are properly the domain of a proactive audit (such as 'the public interest') would undoubtedly negatively affect the effectiveness of the passive financial audit.

A major issue is who sets the criteria by which the corporation's performance is judged. There are clear disadvantages in the criteria being set by the management, the auditor or any specific stakeholder (such as the shareholders). But there is no consensus within society of the meaning of such general terms as 'public interest', 'sustainable' and 'social justice'. In view of this lack of consensus, there is scope for a fundamental rethink of audit.

A fruitful area for active audit

An example of where proactive audit could, in our opinion, add value is for the thousands of mid-ranking companies – that is, between FTSE 350 level and the micro businesses that don't require an audit. In such cases, the auditor could, alongside the audit, provide the general business advice and support so valued by clients, but without the conflict of interest rules that restrict the auditor of a major or PIE company.

Notes

1 Financial scandals: a historical overview, *Accounting and Business Research*, Volume 49, 2019, Issue 5. www.tandfonline.com/doi/full/10.1080/00014788.2019.1610591
2 https://en.wikipedia.org/wiki/McKesson_%26_Robbins_scandal_(1938)
3 https://en.wikipedia.org/wiki/Penn_Central_Transportation_Company
4 https://en.wikipedia.org/wiki/Polly_Peck
5 Robert Maxwell Mirror Group, Bank of Credit Commerce International among others.
6 www.thebalancesmb.com/sarbanes-oxley-act-and-the-enron-scandal-393497
7 https://en.wikipedia.org/wiki/Arthur_Andersen
8 https://en.wikipedia.org/wiki/Arthur_Andersen
9 https://en.wikipedia.org/wiki/Lehman_Brothers
10 www.theguardian.com/global/2011/dec/12/royal-bank-of-scotland-fsa-report
11 https://en.wikipedia.org/wiki/Patisserie_Valerie
12 https://en.wikipedia.org/wiki/Wirecard_scandal
13 www.ft.com/content/7eb26473-96a2-4b07-af02-0c0b7e8b8eda
14 www.london.edu/think/can-regulation-stop-financial-scandals

15 www.frc.org.uk/news/july-2022/sanctions-against-kpmg-and-others-in-connection-wi
16 www.ft.com/content/7911c867-fabe-428d-a5d6-4ec5140e6a7e
17 www.ft.com/content/ab3a30c6-4491-46fc-83cd-812c777c337a
18 Bhaskar et al., *Disruption in the Audit Market: The Future of the Big Four*. Routledge, 2019.
19 www.ft.com/content/7911c867-fabe-428d-a5d6-4ec5140e6a7e
20 www.ft.com/content/2677ce1c-6cb3-4750-be93-7787ef6335b3
21 See Book 2, Bhaskar et al., *Financial Failures & Scandals: From Enron to Carillion*. Routledge, 2019.
22 Cited in Humphrey et al. (1993, p. 57). www.thetimes.co.uk/article/have-we-given-up-on-audit-reform-st2mw5l58
23 Cited in Humphrey et al. (1993, p. 57). Humphrey, C., Moizer, P., and Turley, S. 1992. The audit expectations gap: An empirical investigation. *Accounting and Business Research*. 23, 395–411. Humphrey, C., Moizer, P., and Turley, S. 1992. Protecting against detection: The case of auditors and fraud? *Accounting, Auditing and Accountability Journal* 6, 39–62.
24 www.journalofaccountancy.com/issues/2001/apr/top10auditdeficiencies.html
25 Conway's book.
26 www.sec.gov/comments/265-28/26528-9199096-249728.pdf
27 www2.deloitte.com/global/en/pages/audit/Covid-19/financial-reporting-ecosystem.html
28 Humphrey et al.
29 The Audit Ecosystem: integrating Artificial Intelligence and Expert Systems in the Auditing Domain, M.A Vasarhelyi, Rutgers University, YouTube, 28 May 2015. www.youtube.com/watch?v=hpQ8zlb8zvI
30 www.thecaq.org/news/strengthening-ecosystem-audit-quality-0/
31 Public Accountants Conference, Singapore.
32 Kozlowski, S. (2018), 'An Audit Ecosystem to Support Blockchain-based Accounting and Assurance', Chan, D.Y., Chiu, V. and Vasarhelyi, M.A. (Ed.) *Continuous Auditing* (*Rutgers Studies in Accounting Analytics*), Emerald Publishing Limited, Bingley, pp. 299–313. https://doi.org/10.1108/978-1-78743-413-420181015
33 Such as McCarthy et al.
34 Book 1.
35 www.investopedia.com/articles/forex/042315/beware-these-five-bitcoin-scam.asp
36 https://time.com/nextadvisor/investing/cryptocurrency/common-crypto-scams/

37 Which also has its own ecosystem which it has represented in diagrammatic and textual form: 'This value-creation schematic highlights all the key elements of how IFAC creates and protects value and is based on the IFAC Strategic Plan 2019-20. This diagram is comprehensive, covering all parts of IFAC's ecosystem, and helps IFAC communicate internally and externally and explain our ecosystem'. www.ifac.org/knowledge-gateway/contributing-global-economy/publications/how-ifac-creates-values; www.ifac.org/system/files/publications/files/How-IFAC-Creates-Value.pdf (emphasis added).

38 www.ifac.org/what-we-do/speak-out-global-voice/points-view/achieving-high-quality-audits

39 www.accaglobal.com/gb/en/professional-insights/global-profession/key-developments-audit-profession.html

40 www.icaew.com/insights/viewpoints-on-the-news/2021/nov-2021/icaew-calls-for-frc-to-rethink-changes-to-audit-firm-governance

41 For example, see this Google page: https://scholar.google.co.uk/scholar?q=importance+of+audit+in+financial+statements&hl=en&as_sdt=0&as_vis=1&oi=scholart

42 Not sure the Future if Audit by the RSA?

43 This categorisation developed through discussions with our colleague (and co-author of the three previous books in this series), John Flower.

44 https://en.wikipedia.org/wiki/Audit

6 The problem with passive audits and regulation

In our continuing quest to answer the questions 'How do we make auditing a positive and progressive force for good?', we need to examine further the role of the FRC/ARGA in seeking to improve audit quality.

The relevance of (passive) audits

This is the traditional view of audit in its passive audit form as told by Paul Munter in late 2021:[1]

> As we mark the upcoming twentieth anniversary of the enactment of the Sarbanes-Oxley Act of 2002 ('SOX'),[2] it is critical for all gatekeepers in the financial reporting ecosystem (auditors, management, and their audit committees) to maintain constant vigilance in the faithful implementation of the requirements of SOX by fulfilling their shared responsibilities to continue to produce high quality financial disclosures that are decision-useful to investors and maintain the public trust in our capital markets. An integral part of the faithful implementation of SOX is for audit firms to remain independent of their audit clients and for audit committees to take ownership of their oversight responsibilities with respect to the independent auditor.

Of course this harps back to the passive audit and the gatekeeper theory of audit. This is not what we would like the reader to regard as the function of audit.

DOI: 10.4324/9780429273865-6

When one reads headlines such as: Donald Trump's accountant says financial statements should 'no longer be relied upon' in the FT[3] eyebrows are raised. The FT reported:

> Donald Trump's longtime accountant, Mazars, has told the Trump Organization that a decade of financial statements it helped prepare for the former president should no longer be relied upon.

In 2021 the FT also headlined:[4]

> Overall, 29 per cent of the 103 audits reviewed were deemed below par. The figures were not an aberration. For the past decade, more than one in five audits inspected every year has not met expectations.
>
> [In 2021 the FRC's} annual review of quality at the UK's top seven audit firms reserved its sharpest tongue-lashing for KPMG. Its discovery for the third year running of substandard banking audits by the firm was 'unacceptable', it said.
>
> BDO and Mazars, two of the firms aspiring to break the dominance of accounting's Big Four — Deloitte, EY, KPMG and PwC — were rated worst of the seven for quality.

The actual FRC press release was alarming:

> The 2020/21 results show that nearly one third of audits inspected by the FRC still require improvement.[5]

We think this probably overstates the care and attention all the larger audit firms actually take in their audits. KPMG, in particular, has benefitted from walking away from the German real estate company: Alder.[6] The ICAEW correctly identified the problem of auditors walking away from clients without providing adequate reason. This was in response, belatedly, to the Brydon criticism aimed squarely at the quality of auditor resignation statements with guidance on making them more informative for stakeholders.[7] And Sports Direct had difficulty finding one of the Big Four and eventually landed Mazars as auditors after an acrimonious split from GT.[8]

KPMG has also benefited from publicity about nudging the rewards of its partners towards the ethical mindset. KPMG's partners in the UK have been told they risk forfeiting their share of the £300m proceeds retained from the sales of its pensions and insolvency divisions if they fail to meet ethical standards.[9] This strengthening of the link between partners' behaviour and their financial rewards comes after a string of regulatory fines into KPMG's audit work.

Recent passive audit failures

As known, passive audits have been given a bad review. This goes back to prior to 2004 when the FRC's Accountancy Scheme was first set up after a number of scandals which included The Maxwell companies, Polly Peck, Equitable Life, and BCCI. Then there were a flurry of cases including the Rover Group and HBOS prior to the current clutch of cases discussed in our book: *Financial Failures & Scandals: From Enron to Carillion 2019,* Routledge, 2019.

The cases that stand out after that include Patisserie Valerie (in the UK, auditor GT) where some of the directors allegedly colluded, 1Malaysian Development Berthad (Malaysia involving EY, Deloitte & KPMG)) where corruption took place, Wirecard (Germany, auditor EY), Evergrande (China, auditor PwC) and FTX (US, auditor Armanino and Prager Metis, potential missing $2 billion and/or mistaken liquidly). They are just a few of the recent financial scandals. We found Wirecard interesting from a passive audit viewpoint.

The Irish Times said this of the Wirecard episode:[10]

> In December 2018, just weeks before doubts about one of its most high-profile clients began to circulate widely, the auditor EY Germany decided to investigate Wirecard's operations more closely. It wanted to scrutinise the German fintech group's internal processes for payments settled by outsourcing partners in Asia – an integral part of the business once valued at €24 billion.
>
> EY staff began shopping with online merchants identified as clients of Wirecard's Asian partners. The auditors splashed out on a €9.95 seven-day-subscription to an Asian porn site,

> bought 'coins' for the football video game Fifa 19 worth \$23.08, ordered a breathalyser for €33.45 and spent ¥1,000 on bitcoin.
>
> The shopping trip gave a clean bill of health to the Munich-based group – one of many that EY provided to Wirecard during a decade of working for it. Unfortunately the merchants did not exist. All had been set up by Wirecard executives to dupe the auditors and help disguise what Munich prosecutors now call 'a fraud in the billions'.
>
> A Dubai-based Wirecard executive at the centre of the fraud had helped identify the merchants to be used by EY to test the system – something that should have set off alarm bells at the auditor, says Martin Wambach, the special investigator for a German parliamentary inquiry into the scandal. The EY staff used prepaid cards supplied by Wirecard for the shopping exercise. That enabled executives at the payments group to manipulate the transactions, a separate inquiry found.
>
> It would be another 18 months before EY finally realised that half of Wirecard's revenue and €1.9 billion of company cash linked to the so-called third party acquiring business (TPA) did not exist. The revelations forced the once high-flying German payments provider into insolvency.

This is the sort of narrative for passive auditing that has caused public concern and gives auditing a bad name in general. One can always say one bad apple should not be held as an indication of the entire industry The problem is there are too many bad apples to be ignored.

Carillion

There have been lots of justifications by the Big Four and all their challengers about sticking to what may narrowly be defined as statutory (but passive) audits. If any one may be in doubt over shoddy, incomplete, rushed, mistaken, incorrect and misunderstood work, please look at this reference for the case against KPMG auditor for Carillion.[11] The witness abatements and internal emails are very revealing. Rushed meetings whilst going on holiday. Failure to examine or look at known problematic overseas contracts. Honeymoons and many other excuses come into play. It seems, reading the tribunal, to be worse than any court-room Movie and TV drama.

The Conservative reversal

The FRC/ARGA has expanded. Once Brexit occurred, successive Conservative government's under Boris Johnson, Liz Truss and Rishi Sunak have all declared to want a Brexit dividend by reducing and eradicating EU bureaucracy and regulations. The move to ARGA and tighter regulations flies in the face of this so called Brexit dividend and bonfire of regulations.

The Government white paper referred to earlier provided a legislative backcloth to the formation of ARGA and its growth from the FRC. However, the noises from the government was for less regulation and the legislative programme for ARGA wasn't revealed.

Let's get back to the FRC/ARGA

We know that post-Brexit the rules and regulations, in general, including non- financial, were supposed to be relaxed to make a more attractive business environment. That goes against the current sense as reported by the serious press. The Times made this argument:[12]

> The company [Carillion] was a house of cards, having grown too quickly, racing to take on new contracts, and borrowing too much when revenue was falling. Its demise caused such outrage that it sparked three reviews from three of the most respected figures in financial circles — Sir John Kingman, Sir Donald Brydon and Lord (Andrew) Tyrie — and prompted pledges that the audit industry would be kicked into shape with sweeping new rules and, crucially, a new regulator to stamp out wrongdoing.

Remember that in 2018, the Kingman Review[13] recommended the creation of the ARGA to replace the 'almost powerless' FRC as the regulator. Then in 2019 the Brydon Report[14] recommended sweeping cultural and organisational changes in his report. Tyrie, when he was chairman of the CMA, also said in 2018/2019 that the main accounting firms should split their audit and consulting practices,[15] among a host of other suggestions. The split of audit and consulting divisions has now occurred though it has been left to the individual firms on how they implement and police this division.

ICAEW reaction

Not that we now feel that this split should be supported in a wider examination of the role and scope of audit. Michael Izza, the then CEO (*who retired in March 2024*) of industry body the ICAEW was reported as saying:

> 'If there isn't legislation — if there isn't an all-round, comprehensive package — we are approaching the limits of what can be done voluntarily', said Michael Izza.

And Izza went on to note:[16]

> The mention of audit reform in this Queen's Speech is doubly disappointing. First, the proposed scope of change is modest and, in particular, it constitutes a missed opportunity to address wider issues in corporate governance. This might well end up as the lopsided reform we have consistently warned against.

That modest approach is something that we return to. Is there something better than the set of watered-down proposals set out in the original government white paper?[17] That draft Bill was aimed at establishing a new statutory regulator and governance authority (ARGA); providing new measures to open up the market, including shared audits; enlarging the scope of public interest entities; and giving the new regulator powers to enforce directors' financial reporting duties – including more responsibility for management.[18]

Izza went on to the inevitable sinking of the original plans:

> The second disappointment is more serious: timing. There seems to be no chance that this Bill will pass in the forthcoming parliamentary session, and very little prospect of it doing so in

> the one after that. Three major independent reviews, a White Paper and many public consultations on from the collapse of Carillion and it seems that we are still literally years away from seeing new legislation on the statute book. It is not too late for government to give this the priority it deserves.

Carson Block[19] owner of Muddy Waters[20] writing in the FT opined:[21]

> Despite scandals at Carillion, Patisserie Valerie, NMC Health, Thomas Cook, Eddie Stobart, Ted Baker and other companies, the UK has dropped audit reform from its next legislative programme. Those scandals show that the audit industry is failing to protect investors and employees from malfeasance. It is therefore not unreasonable to state that the audit industry is effectively little more than a tax on companies in service of a white-collar jobs programme.
>
> The root cause of this dysfunction is that audit firms are not held materially accountable for their failures. Large audit firms have created a legal structure — a legal fiction, really — of independent 'member firms' that serve to ringfence liability when something goes wrong. Money and firm personnel move freely through these ringfences, but the auditors have generally been able to convince governments and courts that financial responsibility does not.
>
> The ringfencing of liability is more egregious considering that member firms trade under the (licensed) brands of the large auditors. This arrangement allows auditors to have their cake and eat it too because the member firms are paid for the value of the global brand being stamped on audit reports, but the licensers of that brand bear no liability for misuse of those brands.
>
> The most insidious way that the audit firms abuse public trust in their brands is through consulting services. Consulting services are generally more lucrative than audits.
>
> Frequently, when a company board wants to whitewash accounting, governance and other business problems, they call upon the consulting firms that are branded the same as the audit operations to conduct dubious investigations that miscreant boards then trumpet as an exoneration.

> As short sellers, we have seen this play out numerous times. Other investors are often under the mistaken assumption that these reviews are conducted according to the same standards as audits.
>
> When corporate accounts are highly misleading, but stop just short of legally being fraud, investors can be harmed while the auditors were willing participants. In theory, boards work for the shareholders and auditors work for the board.
>
> Often in the real world, though, management effectively controls boards and therefore the auditors. When companies want to mislead investors and the public about the health of their businesses, auditors can be eager partners, issuing unqualified opinions where often the only discomfort visible is in opaquely written notes to the financial statements that even short sellers can struggle to understand.

This was perhaps as heavy a criticism as any of those in the FT. Usually the FT is more critical of regulation. But there again the FT is not alone. That said Carson Block provides two examples:

a Reverse factoring which is a technique that may allow companies to turn bank borrowings into accounts payable (money owed to suppliers). This decreases a company's apparent leverage and could improve reported cash flow. Block claims that this has played a role in the collapse of several companies including Carillion and NMC Health

b Book gains on asset sales as operating profit. (Block claims this is legal but unethical). Normally such gains would be reported within non-operating profit. He claims, rightly to us, that this can be misleading and manipulates investors' perceptions of profitability.

Block concludes this opinion by writing:

> My hopes for UK audit reform were modest. The UK could have been a leader on this but I've seen the audit industry successfully erode numerous attempts at imposing accountability on it in various jurisdictions, to the point that little, if anything, substantive is done.

> So I am shocked, but not surprised, at how the forces of box-ticking have seemingly snatched another victory for the failing status quo from the jaws of defeat. I am therefore left to lament and remind anyone who listens that if we don't become better stewards of capitalism, capitalism's future is far from assured.

The Times reported in the same article:

> Without clear rules, there is also a risk of a gulf in governance standards between different companies. 'Inevitably, there will be some organisations that say, "Well we don't have to do it, so we won't". So the worst ones don't get better', a senior auditor at a big firm said.
>
> Roger Barker at the Institute of Directors said the FRC would be left 'in limbo' if ARGA was not created. IoD members are frustrated that audit and corporate governance reform 'doesn't appear to be viewed as a priority by the government'.

The problem is that the ARGA/FRC has ramped up its enforcement work, increased its budget and almost doubled its staff numbers in preparation for the launch of the new regulator. Kwasi Kwarteng, ex-BEIS minister chose the former BT chairman, Jan du Plessis as chairman of the FRC in December 2021 to oversee the launch of ARGA. As the FT and the Times have reported,[22] frustration is running high in the City and concerns have been heightened following reports that Sir Jon Thompson, the FRC chief executive who was expected to run ARGA, is to become the chair of HS2. So his attention may be focused on the massive overrun of cost of the HS2 project. That project may also come under fire if the government cuts spending in the 2023 onwards era.

Making passive audited annual reports useful and reliable

One practitioner commented to us that making accounts useful is an old issue – but it has never been satisfactorily dealt with. In general, the response has been to provide more and more information, which is then less and less understandable. The same is true with the longer annual reports with a narrative which is always positive regardless of the underlying reality.

All practitioners would wish to make sure that audited accounts and annual reports are reliable. Again, the general response has been to increase the amount of information – hence the very lengthy audit reports – running to at least six or seven pages – mostly unintelligible to the lay man. A trivial but real example of which is the FRC's annual report where the audit report runs to 14 pages.[23] An audit report needs to be concise and to the point. A further point might be that the audit report is too 'straight-jacketed'. It is either clean or qualified, but little in-between. The format is also too rigid. Some practitioners believe the audit does not need reinventing, but it just needs to ensure that auditors do their work properly.

What has been the ICAEW role in this

The ICAEW seems to have been unable to act appropriately with the big failures. It has been the FRC/ARGA that has been running all the regulations and control of auditing. This is only likely to increase. This leaves all the professional accounting bodies relatively weaker. The ICAEW has probably suffered the most and may now have lost some power, influence, control and even educational standards of the auditing profession.

The FRC/ARGA's position

Ideally auditors would serve a higher ideal and not require regulation. Recent failures have changed that. The focus has been on historical passive audits but we think that this focus is a mistake. Positive proactive auditing should help the firm being audited. Since the original Kingman[24] and other reports there was much seesawing between further FRC/ARGA strengthening and less regulation but with no final decision. To some extent this threw up a dichotomy. If the government's objective is to have less regulation post-Brexit and fewer EU regulations, the ARGA proposals have actually led to more regulations and more form filling than exists anywhere in the EU. So instead of reducing regulation the government has succeed in tightening and increasing regulations. If a company has a choice of where to list it will be less willing to list in the UK because of the increased regulation. The bank's bonuses being lifted may change that marginally for banks. But for the rest, this in turn will impact on hastening the decline of the UK stock markets in relation to our EU counterparts, the US (the big winner for post-Brexit banking in our view) or emerging Asian ones.

Proactive auditing

What the FRC has fundamentally reinforced is its concept that regulations are something a company has to do – not something that is good for the company.

Above all, our worry is that auditing and the audit market are now facing disruption with no positive or beneficial signs emerging in terms of impact on companies, reporting, investors, auditors or the audit market.

Audit is still typically seen as a necessary evil and not something that helps a company. There ought to be a fundamental rethink. Which is what we now try to encourage through our proposal for proactive auditing.

Notes

1 www.sec.gov/news/statement/munter-audit-2021-10-26
2 *See* Sarbanes-Oxley Act of 2002, 15 U.S.C. 7211, *Pub. L. 107-204. 750 Stat. 116. 30 July 2002*, available at www.congress.gov/bill/107th-congress/house-bill/3763/text.
3 www.ft.com/content/09c4e4b7-3631-4e00-8455-11b07f9b8012
4 www.ft.com/content/3ef7de69-5dfd-4f45-88da-c3b74384979b
5 www.frc.org.uk/news/july-2021/frc-annual-audit-quality-inspection-results-2020-2
6 www.ft.com/content/e9210bc8-a9f4-4169-b69a-0cd4fe9508de
7 www.icaew.com/insights/viewpoints-on-the-news/2022/apr-2022/auditor-resignation-statements-why-clarity-is-vital
8 www.theguardian.com/business/2019/oct/23/sports-direct-appoints-new-auditor-split-grant-thornton-rsm
9 www.ft.com/content/2677ce1c-6cb3-4750-be93-7787ef6335b3
10 www.irishtimes.com/business/financial-services/wirecard-and-ey-germany-the-anatomy-of-a-flawed-audit-1.4710898
11 www.frc.org.uk/getattachment/e3fa9c9f-ea20-4474-81b0-ce6228ea0146/KPMG-Regenersis-and-Carillion-AQR-Tribunal-Report-27-09-22.pdf
12 www.thetimes.co.uk/article/have-we-given-up-on-audit-reform-st2mw5l58

13 See www.gov.uk/government/publications/financial-reporting-council-review-2018
www.gov.uk/government/publications/the-quality-and-effectiveness-of-audit-independent-review
www.gov.uk/government/publications/financial-reporting-council-review-2018
14 www.gov.uk/government/publications/the-quality-and-effectiveness-of-audit-independent-review
www.gov.uk/government/publications/the-quality-and-effectiveness-of-audit-independent-review
15 www.gov.uk/government/consultations/statutory-audit-services-initial-consultation-on-the-competition-and-markets-authority-recommendations
16 www.icaew.com/insights/viewpoints-on-the-news/2022/may-2022/queens-speech-delivers-lopsided-reform-on-audit
17 www.gov.uk/government/consultations/restoring-trust-in-audit-and-corporate-governance-proposals-on-reforms
18 www.icaew.com/insights/viewpoints-on-the-news/2022/may-2022/queens-speech-delivers-lopsided-reform-on-audit
19 Chief Investment Officer of Muddy Waters LLC, an investment research and short seller. Often known for their whistleblowing reports. Carson Block is reported as owner when Googled.
20 Muddy Waters has been involved in highlighting a number of financial scandals. These include Burford Capital, NMC Heath and Luckin Coffee, see https://en.wikipedia.org/wiki/Muddy_Waters_Research
21 www.ft.com/content/7afea69e-c924-4863-a595-a45cbfba419e
22 See www.ft.com/content/ef21aaf2-28f2-442a-8d6f-e5b3ff5599f5; www.thetimes.co.uk/article/have-we-given-up-on-audit-reform-st2mw5l58
23 Audited by the National Audit Office (Greg Wilson) we presume using FRC principles. www.frc.org.uk/getattachment/8caee6b0-0fe0-4489-9edc-96e24a27d277/FRC-Annual-Report-and-Accounts-2021-22.pdf
24 https://assets.publishing.service.gov.uk/government/uploads/system/uploads/attachment_data/file/767387/frc-independent-review-final-report.pdf

7 Making audit a positive and progressive force for good

Promoting the proactive audit

With respect to what it would entail for audit to become a positive and progressive force for good there are quite a few easy things to agree on. For example, an auditor's investigation and report has to be based on a comprehensive evidence base. Similarly, an auditor has to ensure that the insight provided through the audit is appropriately constructed – which may require, depending on the circumstances, a very sceptical or a more enabling attitude to dominate the auditor's thinking and analysis. In some cases, this will demand an exacting interrogation of management; in others it can entail a more discursive and catalytic approach that encourages managerial development.

As auditors are paid (and paid quite substantially), it is inherently difficult to represent its value solely in terms of being unbiased or neutral. As such, we have to acknowledge that the value of an audit is capable of resting on other factors and contributions. We need to embrace a more dynamic definition of audit that places the emphasis less on predetermined input criteria and qualifications and more on the output and outcomes associated with an audit – such as the contribution it makes in terms of the quality of its insight, of being a positive and progressive force for good, for the benefit of the audited entity and society. This may well mean that we have to be less concerned with the separation of audit and consulting services and more centred on bolstering among auditors their sense of professionalism and commitment to serving the public interest.

Similarly, we need to move beyond regulatory reforms such as joint or managed shared audits as they are not advancing the

DOI: 10.4324/9780429273865-7

essential purpose of audit but would make the process of the current form of audit more complex and more expensive.

Dynamic definition

We are very much in agreement with developing efforts and a growing body of literature calling for a conceptual reconfiguration of audit (e.g. see Humphrey et al., 2021; 2024; Adams et al., 2024). We also agree with accompanying claims that such reconfiguration is better placed to bolster audit professionalism than more, increasingly intrusive, regulation.

Interpreting and building on such literature, we offer the following observations and opinions:

- Current policy commitments to regulation and standard setting are misguided, damaging to professionalism and unlikely to deliver fundamental innovation;
- Such commitments need to be assessed more directly in terms of achievements/impact. They (and so many previous 'much needed and vital' regulatory reforms) have not restored trust and confidence in audit;
- The profession seems somewhat 'off the pace' and not leading the type of reform developments that really could make a significant difference. They seem too centred on not upsetting regulators and acting as regulators themselves;
- Talk of 'future ready professionals' by various professional bodies (such as IFAC) understates the creative opportunities for development in the role of accounting and audit.
- For the long terms best interests of the profession and the public, we would like to see national and international accounting and audit bodies acting less as followers and more as leaders;
- In particular, the profession has to recognise that for all the talk of the social significance and importance of audit, various policy think tanks (such as the Brookings Institute or the British Academy) typically place a quite limited emphasis on audit when discussing policy priorities in reforming or reinventing the corporation and delivering a better society;
- We also need to understand better why there has been such a delay in implementing audit reform and why opportunities to

advance the nature and significance of audit as a concept have not been seized.

Put very directly, an audit expectations gap is not longstanding without good reason but the answer does not lie in ever more external regulation – not least when regulatory efforts seem to be centred (or stuck) on trying to restore trust in the same old audit. If we are really to move beyond the audit expectations gap and a static representation of audit, then the profession has to take greater responsibility for the conceptual advancement of audit and demonstrating the resulting societal and economic benefits of such a transformation. As others have stressed (see Brydon,[1] Humphrey[2]), there are major opportunities for the advancement of audit professionalism through a broader representation of the purpose of audit, arguably increasing the relevance of audit not just to investors but to a much broader group of stakeholders as discussed by the ICAEW.[3]

This has to be where the profession has a competitive knowledge advantage and it should not be waiting, dependent on those outside of the profession to advise on how best to develop the scope and purpose of audit. If anything, it is here, this level of jurisdictional authority and respect, that fundamentally distinguishes between a strong profession and a strong regulator. As Humphrey (2021) emphasised:

> 'I see much agreement in the need for a strong regulator and much expectation that once this is established so much more will follow. However, do the roots of a strong profession really depend so centrally on the existence of a strong regulator? How much more important is the knowledge that the professional function you are providing is strong, sound and widely acknowledged and respected for its economic and social purposefulness – and not plagued by concerns that it is misunderstood or misconceived ... If we sidestep key conceptual issues, they will come back in a haunting manner, most probably when the next set of major corporate collapses breaks, and questions are asked as to how such things happened under the watch of a much bigger and more powerful regulator?'.

Seizing such opportunities demands a different form of thinking, adopting what Humphrey et al.[4] classified as a more dynamic reconfiguration of audit. Our direct response to such calls is the notion of a proactive audit – which we believe can move us significantly beyond a historical obsession with the audit expectations gap. It is the antithesis of a static representation of audit and can directly enable the profession to lead audit reform and to make the societal benefits of audit more visible. If the societal aim is, post-Covid, one of 'building back better', then we believe that audit as a concept has to be more broadly specified.

The way forward for a proactive audit

We start from the core premise that a pro-active audit should be beneficial to the company or entity being audited. It should not be a function represented in largely 'negative' terms or spirit. Rather than being portrayed as a 'necessary evil', an irritating disturbance or even an irrelevance, audit should be represented as a progressive force for good, for a better future. As such, it is very important here to recognise that vital to notions of audit being 'proactive' is the spirit through which we represent and talk about audit. The priority at this stage is not one of formal, detailed definition. Instead, it is one of mindset. We need to think more of what audit can do, what it change, what it can contribute – rather than what it cannot do, or what is not audit. Being 'proactive' starts with a positive outlook – that audit is and will achieve something distinctive.

The second, related, core dimension of a proactive audit is that audit is not represented in a static fashion. Audit should be dynamic and always capable of evolution, both conceptually and practically – a function: that adapts to the specific circumstances and contexts it encounters; that responds and develops to secure particular outcomes and impacts.

Combining the two dimensions of spirit and application can be done in different ways and to different levels – reflecting varying levels of ambition and scale of pursued change. For instance, a commitment for the audit function to be reliably useful could mean providing greater scope for less standardised audit reporting, – incorporating considerations of how to simplify the audit report or alternatively how to make it more granular than a binary pass-fail assessment. This may also mean that more detailed audit metrics (including a breakdown of audit hours by seniority of audit team personnel) become a vivid part of an audit report. An alternative and potentially more novel approach might be to view the audit less as a confrontation to management and more as a process of collaboration where a committed and trusted management team can learn proactively from the broader experiences and insights of auditors who have gained valuable sector specific knowledge from other audit assignments. Press headlines are typically dominated by examples of friction between management and auditors (for recent examples at the back end of 2022 – see the cases of De La Rue,[5] Carr[6] and Clarks[7] over going concern warnings and delays in the reporting of annual results). But a pro-active audit could also be collaborative and enabling in its approach and contribution. While we have, in regulatory terms, become centred on separating audit from other 'non-audit' services capable of being provided by professionally qualified audit teams, conceiving of audit in more proactive terms can serve to disturb or reconfigure the boundaries we draw around audit, assurance and consulting (for more discussion, see Humphrey et al., 2021; 2024). A proactive audit could be much more forward looking in its orientation (rather than being primarily historical) with a commitment to helping a company to improve, especially if it is not doing well and unsure as to why it is underperforming. Thinking of audit in proactive terms also means placing less emphasis on standardisation. Instead of thinking of audits through increasing standardisation, we should think of audits in terms of making a difference and different contexts and circumstances will demand different forms of and ways of conducting an audit. Or in terms of the way the Brydon report framed the purpose of auditing, we should start thinking of framing and undertaking audits in ways that have the best possible chance of building and maintaining deserved confidence in the audited company, its directors and the information it makes public.

Thinking more positively and proactively about what audit can do and achieve also immediately opens up the scope for the development of audit professionalism – in essence, it encourages a switch away from the regulation of an existing function that we know is not meeting expectations to the professionalisation of a reconfigurated audit that offers something new and dynamic. Connectedly, this also gives a broader foundation for what seems increasingly essential – namely, the need for a separate audit profession with appropriate intellectual and practical training. In this respect, we agree with the spirit of the recommendations in the Brydon report and see much promise in a separate professional body with its own syllabus and examinations. There is a growing realisation that the roots of a strong profession have to rest in something more than the establishment of a strong regulator (e.g. see Humphrey et al., 2024. As a profession, auditors should be arguing that they need to be central in driving reform initiatives and maintaining suitable quality control standards. If an auditing profession does not see the future of audit as resting in its hands, it is unlikely to be a major driving force in audit innovation.

In this regard, we would argue that the pursuit of a more proactive audit necessitates the development of a more proactive profession. The two should go hand in hand with the first step being to recognise the importance of ensuring that audit reform does not just concentrate on reforming the regulation of audit. Audit reform led by forward thinking audit professionals genuinely committed to working in the public interest can deliver something much more profound than a reform process centred on the regulation of a fixed or predetermined form of audit. A truly proactive audit profession would not let reform be something that others do to the profession; rather it is something that should be led by the profession.

Taking the lead in audit reform also does not mean accepting reforms on the grounds of political necessity, without knowing if they 'work' and are capable of delivering intended effects and outcomes. It means being willing to experiment and to recognise that what works in certain circumstances may not work as well in others. There is much talk at present of the importance of having an 'improvement regulator' but surely 'improvement' is something that a profession should be taking responsibility for itself. Let's talk about a profession committed to improvement and advancement rather than a profession that looks to the regulator to specify the best ways forward. The UK government is looking for individual companies to develop their own Audit and Assurance Policy statements and for a subsequent development of the market for assuring financial and non-financial information beyond the financial statements. This gives the profession a vivid opportunity to take the lead regarding the future development of audit and audit purpose – and, thereby, demonstrate its professional 'strength' through experimentation and innovation.

The need for more dynamism in audit reform does not just come from the demand side but also the supply side. There are persistent signals that auditing is no longer seen as an attractive career – we not only have audit firms walking away from clients that are perceived to be too risky (in terms of the likelihood of accounting misstatement), but we have auditors (both senior and junior) choosing to pursue careers in others parts of the accounting profession and/or business world because the latter are seen to offer greater personal development opportunities with less personal risk. Conceptual innovation has to make audit a more attractive, professional career path; the predominant development path has to become one where audit is something that people want to do rather than avoid or get out of.

In this regard, we welcome efforts to get people thinking differently about audit (see Humphrey et al., 2021; 2024) and see our own emphasis on proactive auditing as being an additional lens through which to pursue an alternative reform trajectory. We need a design-mindset to audit reform[8] (ICAEW, 2021) that is not 'regulatory-centric' but 'audit-centric' in its approach[9] (Hatherly, 2022). We agree that this type of approach, centred on what audit could become, has an inherently greater sense of professional attractiveness than the traditional focus on the auditing expectations gap and what auditing cannot be expected to do.

Sir Donald Brydon did recommend in his report that ARGA should act as the midwife to create a new profession of auditing (para. 6.0.11), but in a subsequent interview, he went on to stress that there is a lot in his report that can be pursued without waiting for legislation, calling for a mindset change: 'I'm rather hoping somebody will stand up and say, "Let's not wait for legislation. Why don't we set up this new profession ourselves and just get on with it?" '[10]

We recognise the challenging nature of such thinking, especially when a prominent counter argument is for auditors merely to concentrate on what they are formally required to do; to do the basic audit well rather than imagining new audit forms. We also know that this is an institutional environment characterised by persistent instability, such that just when it feels that there is a space for calm reflection and innovative thinking, fire-fighting activities are called on as the next corporate scandal breaks, implicates the major audit firms and breathes life into the same old criticisms and laments. We can see such a consequential tendency in the way that key institutional players at one moment in time look more openly committed to broader reform but then get pushed back to taking rather more conservative positions.[11]

At a time when so much prominence has been attached to business and societal regeneration, of 'building back better' and to best effect, the profession has to be looking actively at moving beyond a defensive battle of self-preservation, of muddling through until the next crisis hits. This is not as 'good as it gets' and a professional priority has to be about preserving a space for the conceptual advancement of audit, of determining how and what forms of auditing can best serve what is determined to be the public interest.

So what is a proactive audit?

At this point, lets review what we mean by proactive audit. We are not saying it is the final answer for the way forward for audit reform but we present it as a catalyst for a wide ranging review. We recognise that this requires the auditor to work closely with management whilst still taking an independent approach and, where necessary, caveating comments to limit liability

Our concept of proactive audit includes:

- it should address the wider group of stakeholders and act as a programme for good for society in general.
- it should offer a granular opinion, that is, not straightjacketed into a binary pass or fail verdict, but reflect on a range of valuation outcomes and business options.
- it should be forward looking, discuss key business risks (and opportunities) and give readers sufficient information for them to come to an informed opinion themselves of the potential for the future development of the company.

Notes

1 https://assets.publishing.service.gov.uk/government/uploads/system/uploads/attachment_data/file/852960/brydon-review-final-report.pdf
2 Humphrey et al., 2021.
3 www.icaew.com/insights/viewpoints-on-the-news/2021/jan-2021/the-brydon-report-and-the-critical-significance-of-its-conceptualisation-of-audit.
4 Humphrey et al., 2021.
5 www.thetimes.co.uk/article/de-la-rue-attacks-auditor-over-going-concern-warning-x8prcsf77
6 www.thetimes.co.uk/article/carrs-delays-results-after-questions-over-audit-0klq5fr57
7 www.thetimes.co.uk/article/auditors-in-new-warning-over-future-of-clarks-ccdcnsc7n
8 ICAEW, 2021.
9 Hatherly, 2022.
10 www.icas.com/insight/trust/sir-donald-brydon-interview-future-of-audit
11 For instance, there is quite a degree of contrast between the lower scale of commitment to conceptual development of audit in the ICAEW's formal 2021 response to the BEIS White Paper which lays stress on reinforcing strengths (www.icaew.com/insights/viewpoints-on-the-news/2021/jul-2021/beis-white-paper-five-steps-crucial-to-deliver-reform; www.icaew.com/-/media/corporate/files/technical/icaew-representations/2021/icaew-rep-6321-restoring-trust-in-audit-and-corporate-governance.ashx?la=en and the reshaping, (re) design mindset, commitments of its 2020 audit manifesto declaration (www.icaew.com/insights/viewpoints-on-the-news/2020/nov-2020/a-manifesto-for-audit)

8 Postscript and thoughts to ponder

Krish Bhaskar, the lead author, was in process of completing this book when he became seriously ill in January 2023 and, very sadly, passed away in April 2023. This last chapter is written as a post-script, as a way of capturing Bhaskar's residing thoughts and to highlight some subsequent developments in the audit practice arena that relate to key points covered in the main body of the book.

Reorganisation

Limited internal restructuring of the various business sections of the large accounting firms (i.e. audit, tax, consultancy, advisory) was dramatically outshone by the proposed total splitting off audit into a separate firm under EYs Project Everest proposals. However, after 18 months of international consultation throughout the firm, Project Everest was cancelled in April 2023, following notable opposition from US partners. There has subsequently been press comment that some form of restructuring may take place but recent reference to the scale of incurred liabilities of over $700m must cast considerable doubt on the main project being resurrected Meanwhile, the major firms in the UK are well advanced in the process of operationally separating their audit and consultancy divisions in response to demands from the FRC for the firms to separate audit and non-audit by 30/9/24. They are also re-examining their governance structures, for example, with a board to oversee management and approve strategy and by the establishment of public oversight boards/panels within the firms.

Little progress on developing joint audits appears to have been made, perhaps reflecting a broader lack of enthusiasm for such

DOI: 10.4324/9780429273865-8

a functional approach. Consideration here can also extend to the potential for new entrants to the audit industry and whether calls for greater choice in the audit market will be matched by a growth in larger scale audit providers? Will the big tech companies see this as a lucrative market, possibly in partnership with an accounting firm?

Turning to the wider accountancy market, James Dow, head of DSW based in NW England, believes that the accountancy sector is on the verge of a tectonic shift. Firms like his own, a disruptor dealing in corporate finance for the SME sector using a franchise model, are examples of the continued shakeup in the sector which could encourage more start–ups, larger specialist firms and more new business models. He says that, while there will always be a place for the big four, the landscape could soon look very different. The result could be a more vibrant marketplace with more diversity and greater choice for professionals and clients alike. Private equity has also invested into professional accounting firms, e.g. Evelyn Partners was built up through a series of mergers between investment management and professional service companies. In 2020, Warburg Pincus came on board as an investor, providing capital to finance a merger between Tilney and accountancy firm Smith & Williamson. The push to invest in AI and other tech has prompted many to bring in outsiders with deep pockets. The sector could look very different in 5 years time!

Technology

The major firms are evidently devoting considerable resources to investigating and implementing new technologies – including generative AI, blockchain, open banking and analytic tools (with developing technology being the subject for many seminars and papers). Alongside this, there is an accompanying need to ensure auditors acquire the skills to assess the opportunities and risks of using generative AI, although it can be argued that the traditional accountancy skills of questioning, scepticism and applying professional judgement should be of paramount importance in this new era.

Relooking at the concept of audit

Throughout this book the fundamental concept of audit has been questioned and suggestions made for some possible alternatives – the proactive audit could be one approach to adding value to the audit process in comparison with the traditional passive style of audit. If audit is to be a proactive force for good, there needs to be a wide-ranging review with all stakeholders to ensure that changes meet the needs of business, the profession and the general public.

One method that would go a long way to avoiding more financial scandals would be to encourage/require a higher degree of curiosity/common sense/scepticism in both audit teams and boardrooms – and that, in itself, might avoid a whole range of formalistic procedures and nip a problem in the bud. For example, just think about how this could have helped to avoid the Post Office scandal in the UK that has been the subject of so much attention recently.

Governments do seem to have dragged their heels in terms of enacting the significant reforms that were recommended following the three major reviews on audit and corporate governance reform. The ICAEW, through its AuditFutures project, has for the past 10 years or so sought to articulate a vision for audit and a better society. One of its outputs was the Audit Manifesto of November 2020 which dealt with how to build a modern audit profession. In an effort to reignite the reform discussion, Sellers co-hosted a high-level seminar in late 2022 at the Alliance Manchester Business School and subsequently wrote providing feedback to the Business Minister Kevin Hollinrake, stressing the importance of implementing substantive and effective reforms.

Draft regulatory proposals were published in July 2023 for new corporate reporting requirements for very large UK companies, including an annual resilience statement to be included in the company's strategic report, as recommended in the Brydon report and supported by unpublished research that has concluded that resilience statements illuminate a way towards responsible, sustainable and adaptable governance with the overriding commitment to building a better world for the public and society.

U turn(s)

Many would very much support such a move as, without adding a mass of data, it would place responsibility firmly on a company's directors, supported by auditors applying professional judgement. However, on 16 October 2023, the

Conservative government withdrew the July draft new reporting regulations following a consultation with senior business leaders/representatives, stressing instead the importance of avoiding burdensome regulation and establishing a more targeted, simpler and effective framework for both business and investors. The announcement was accompanied by supportive comments from business but more recent items in the press suggest there is groundswell of pressure for the government to speed up audit reform to stave off further high profile corporate collapses.

The Conservative government, while stressing its intent to reduce regulatory burdens and pressures and to make the UK one of the best places in the world to do business, did still state that it remained committed to wider audit and corporate governance reform, including establishing ARGA to replace the existing FRC. Legislation was promised in order to deliver these reforms when Parliamentary time allows. However, in documents filed after the November 2023 autumn statement, there was yet another U turn, with the then Business and Trade Secretary, Kemi Badenoch, stating that the government would not proceed with plans to create ARGA. She outlined the FRC's new remit, stressing that proportionality of any new requirements is essential and that unnecessary red tape should be reduced in order to enhance UK economic growth and its international competitiveness.[1] [2]

The new Labour government in July 2024 included a bill for Audit and Regulatory Reform (including replacing the FRC with ARGA) in the first tranche of bills it intends to bring to Parliament – no doubt we will learn in due course whether or not this includes fundamental review or ends up being watered down as the bill goes through the legislative process.

FRC

The FRC's 2023 audit quality report showed some marginal improvement amongst the largest firms. However, with audit fees increasing by 14% overall (and possibly 50% more for complex audits) – reflecting the increased regulatory work required – it remains a live question as to whether audit quality is commensurately improving and delivering suitable cost-beneficial consequences for audited companies and their key stakeholders.

Richard Moriarty, the CEO of the FRC, together with chairman Sir Jan du Plessis, certainly have a challenging task to continue the transformation of FRC along the lines initially envisaged for ARGA – but also now have the additional responsibility of delivering better/improvement regulation to support growth for corporate Britain. Just listing out the collective achievement of tough targets, smarter rules, reducing red tape, keeping the UK attractive to business, delivering enhanced levels of corporate governance and better businesses gives a very clear indication of the enormity of the intentions – even without acknowledging that a good many of them could well run in contrasting directions and imply competing commitments. In short, a lot is being asked of regulation but can it deliver, especially when certain changes and reforms are deemed as falling out of scope? In January 2024, the FRC announced several revisions to the UK Corporate Governance Code with the stated aim of seeking to 'enhance transparency and accountability of UK plc and help to support the growth and competitiveness of the UK and its attractiveness as a place to invest. The revisions include a stronger focus on internal controls with Boards required to explain through a declaration in their Annual Reports how they have done this and the conclusions reached'.[3] Critics are likely to claim that this looks like a somewhat watered down version of the previously promised requirement for Boards to produce substantial Resilience Statements and that such 'watering down' is too late in the day to prevent leading PLCs from shifting their main share listings away from London? A tone of analysis underlain with the anticipation that the FRC, in whatever institutional form it ends up, is going to struggle to please a substantive some, let alone everyone. A conclusion that, in turn, poses the question as to what responsibility for driving reform needs to be picked up by the accounting profession?

Competition

According to the FRC, it is vital that the audit industry is competitive to preserve the integrity of financial information in capital markets. However, the low number of audits of listed companies undertaken by mid-tier firms has led to concerns over the lack of competition within the audit sector. The Big Four currently accounts for 98% of FTSE 350 audits.[4] Concerns over investigations by the FRC into mid-tier audit firms undertaking listed company work have made it more difficult and expensive for these firms to get the professional indemnity coverage necessary for auditing listed companies. Lengthy investigations by the FRC and the possibility of large fines from the FRC also means that insurers of audit firms may have to increase insurance premiums.

It has been argued that the FRC is in a challenging position of needing to ensure that audit standards stay high whilst balancing that with the need to make pitching for listed company audits worthwhile for mid-tier accountancy firms. One thing mid-market firms can proactively do to reduce the risk of manual errors is to make better use of technology. And, when adopted in a thoughtful way, technology can give these firms greater capacity to take on larger audits, and the confidence to compete for them.

The FRC has been visibly instructed by the government to address the lack of competition in the audit market and a consultation process commenced in 2024 – it remains interesting to be seen if anything useful emerges from such a process but, again the challenge is a profound one – requiring regulatory initiatives to confront and counter market forces that have persistently resulted in the market being dominated by a small number of powerful audit providers. Again, maybe the time has come where attempts to open up the audit market to new providers has to allow for more conceptual diversity in the product being delivered.

Fines

The value of fines issued by the FRC against auditors rose by 29% (in the year to 31 August 2023), from £21m to £27m. The increase in number of fines has been driven by an uptick in fines levied against the Big Four accountancy firms from 14 in 2021/22 to 19 in 2022/23. Over recent years the FRC has stepped up its use of fines as part of its efforts to improve the quality of audits and the regulator has also more than doubled the size of its enforcement team from just 14 in 2020 to 64 in 2022.

A further step change occurred in October 2023, when it was reported that KPMG has been awarded a record £21m fine from the FRC over 'exceptional failings' in its audit of Carillion ahead of the firm's 2018 collapse. The FRC imposed a fine of £26.5m, reduced by 30% to £18.55m to reflect the firm's co-operation and admissions with regards to the investigation opened on 26 January 2018 into the statutory audit of the financial statements of Carillion for the financial years ended 31 December 2014, 2015 and 2016 and additional audit work in 2017. Substantial fines were also imposed on two (former) KPMG partners.

For some these figures are massive and represent an increasingly active and tough regulator. For others, the amounts are dwarfed by the sheer scale of revenues being generated by the big firms. On another dimension, there is the risk that such fines are increasingly inevitable given the uncertainties attached to any audit (the current audit opinion, after all, is a definitive opinion based on a probabilistic methodology – where there is an accepted risk of error). If regulatory fines are treated by firms as simply another cost of operating rather than a serious wake-up call to transform their ways of conducting audits, then radically positive changes are not going to happen. Rather to the contrary, fines levied on individual partners – or even other, more junior, staff – can have a serious demotivating effect and may lead to the pursuit of other, less risky and more rewarding career paths (such as management consulting) – making it more difficult to attract and retain high quality and skilled auditors and, longer term, having a negative impact on future ruling levels of audit quality. Or will such tendencies be dominated by the frequent assertions on the part of the big firms that they are an engine for both economic growth and social mobility (with people such as Kevin Ellis, former senior partner of PwC's UK and Middle East alliance, being awarded the CBE in the 2023/24 for New Years Honours List 'for service to economic growth and expanding social mobility')?

So, what moves for audit reform can we expect?

Firstly, lets review some specific developments underway:

- The FRC published in March 2024 its plan and budget for 2024–25.[5] It emphasises its role in supporting UK businesses to grow and thrive while delivering on its core public interest responsibilities – but given the delay to legislation including to establish ARGA, it has decided not to increase its headcount as had been envisaged if its remit had been expanded.

- The FRC is consulting re the lack of competition in the audit market
- The ICAEW continues to press for the reform agenda to be reinstated as a government priority. On p. 30 in the Trust section of its Manifesto 2024–25, it states 'Significant development of the government's reform package has taken place and legislation should be nearly ready to go'.[6] The ICAEW goes on to state 'A proper and fresh review of the proposals is now needed as a final stage before their adoption' – a statement fully endorsed in this book, providing that that review is not just 'proper and fresh' but also looks at the fundamental concept of audit.
- An International Standard for the Audit of Less Complex Entities (ISA for LCE), issued by the International Auditing and Assurance Board (IAASB) is set to be effective for audits starting from 15/12/25.[7] Its objective is to provide the same level of assurance, reasonable assurance, but with tailored and proportionate approach to the unique audit needs of less complex entities. It is a risk-based approach, principles-based and has an intuitive structure. However, before the standard can be used in jurisdictions, each jurisdiction must decide whether to adopt it.

Secondly, looking further ahead and, while not exactly aligning with the notion of 'who dares wins', it is very evident that the future development path for audit is one that could go in some very contrasting directions. The immediate one to address from the last 5–6 years of official inquiries into the quality of audit and its future, is whether the UK government is capable of enacting sufficiently radical reforms to restore trust and confidence in the audit process? And what counts as sufficient and/or necessary?

The jury is not only still out on the first question and likely to be a hung one for both whenever an opinion is given. The question that can be answered is that there is a real opportunity to enact radical reform of audit – but for this to happen we have to think beyond the current conception of audit. Paul Stephenson, UK managing partner for audit and assurance at Deloitte, expressed in a November 2023 article in the Times when he stressed that the key to restoring trust and confidence in the audit process does not lie in piecemeal or lopsided changes but to create, in partnership with all the stakeholders, an overarching vision, with the Government committed to implementing it. However, of fundamental importance here is that, the pursuit of restoring confidence must not just treat the current form of audit as fixed, nor regard the focus of reform as being one of reassurance that the current form of audit is the best we can have. Similarly, now is not the time after so many official investigations to shift the reform focus away from audit to other elements or dimensions of corporate governance. Yes they are and can be very important – but 'audit' reform has to mean reform of 'audit'. People interested in audit reform have to do more than set out with the good intentions of securing change (although it is also sure that a good number are seriously intent on maintaining the status quo) – they have to carry things through to the delivery of substantive change. In this regard, substantive means that audit has to be seen as a function that is open not just to restoration but also reconfiguration – or what Humphrey et al. (2021) have classified as a process of dynamic repair.

So what is it that makes people either inherently against change or to lose the momentum for or commitment to change in the audit arena? What stops them from thinking differently or pursuing something new and distinctive? These are questions that Bhaskar was definitely contemplating and wanting not only to address but to resolve in writing this last part of the book. Maybe he was being too optimistic and not giving due recognition to the classic audit expectations gap terminology of '*plus ca change, plus c'est la meme chose*'. Or was it his great sense of optimism and commitment that the audit reform arena desperately lacks? Whatever the correct position is here, Bhaskar would have been greatly concerned by the faltering level and nature of 'progress', especially given his passionate belief in the capacity of new technology to drive change in the profession. Furthermore, it is the profession and its professional values and responsibilities that he would have chosen to prioritise and emphasise in his speeches and his writing. He was not someone who wanted to believe that the future of the profession should or has to reside in the hands of regulators – and if that has become the case, then this is very much a self-inflicted diminishment in the social standing and significance of the profession.

Thirdly and crucially

Let's take the opportunity after the moves to deregulation and lack of action for effective reform, to take a fundamental rethink to the whole situation.

Audit has continued almost unchanged since the 19th century but now in the 21st century, we should be recognising and responding to the major changes and priorities that are taking place in the corporate world. This includes the importance of ESG (Environmental, Social and Governance) but especially companies' responsibilities to all stakeholders including the community at large. The proactive audit (see Chapter 7) has the potential to contribute as the questions being asked of business are wider and require deeper analysis and reflection than that provided by a traditional, financial statements 'audit'.

I am not an academic but, hopefully, as a pragmatic businessman, I look at all the developments (or lack of) I have seen over the past few years and believe we should encourage and empower the future leaders of our audit profession to take up the challenge by promoting discussion – and let them start with a clean piece of paper.

The developments highlighted on the previous page are only tinkering at the edges. Let's mull over some more fundamental ideas:

- Most importantly of all, should there first be a full and public discussion of what an audit is in the modern world so that the general public has increased clarity and understanding of the process?
- In my business experience with SMEs, I found companies appreciated the value-added services that an auditor can bring including from experience from other clients. The smallest clients, many of them with turnover below £10.2m (possibly increasing to £15m in future) are potentially exempt from audit but benefit from a continuing relationship with the previously named auditor, many of whom now badge themselves as 'Business Advisers'. Why can't these services be offered to SMEs, subject to the firms ensuring there is no conflict (either

actually or by perception) between the audit and other service lines?

- The clear independence of the audit team from the other services provided by the professional firm may be important for FTSE 100 and major international firms but this may not be relevant for a number of mid-market companies, especially those deemed to be Public Interest Entities (PIE). Would the proactive audit process harness the wider supportive role of the auditor, whilst still exercising independence in forming the audit opinion?
- In Manchester the legacy company from the now defunct Manchester Society of Chartered Accountants is endeavouring to support radical thinking by university students by financially supporting some students and staff at three major universities in Greater Manchester. Topics researched in their dissertations include the impact of AI on audit, efforts to rebrand the image of accountancy plus developing a skill set for ESG/CSR as part of the audit process. Would a proactive audit possibly help to highlight problems to management at an early stage, for example, modern slavery or environmental concerns in the supply chain before the situation becomes public and potentially harmful to the company?
- Moving to the national level, should the profession take over from regulators to give leadership to these changes – perhaps the ICAEW could establish a Research Institute, following on from the ICAEW's 2020Audit Manifesto, but with a broader remit than the AuditFutures programme to produce a strong reforming agenda. Could this strengthen the case for the auditors to design positive processes rather than the limiting/restricting actions resulting from excessive regulation?
- Indeed, some commentators propose a form of light touch regulation – could there be greater emphasis on encouraging professional judgment and valuable skill sets rather than publicising sanctions on audit staff (below partner level) and only publishing bad practices without also highlighting good practices?

Let's look at some possible significant amendments to the audit process:

- Would a granular audit opinion with appropriate explanations be of more help to the investor than a straight choice between a Clean or Qualified opinion?
- Whilst audit may often be considered poor value and expensive, should there be a wider use of certificates, akin to reporting accountants' reports, be offered in relation to value added services, pre-investment reviews, ESG matters, etc., where the legal liabilities of the reporting accountant can be limited?
- It may take AI several years to be successfully integrated into the audit process but can this be achieved without compromising the overriding importance of applying professional judgement and scepticism?

Our young people, when unrestrained by precedent or hierarchical structures, can have the vision with a clarity of purpose to cut through complexities. As our profession is over 150 years old, surely it is time for reinvention of our purposes and methods in a way to meet the demands of stakeholders in the 21st century.

Krish Bhaskar had both a *'passion for learning and a yearning for change'*. Hopefully readers of this book will accept the challenges presented by its analysis and help to close any inevitable gaps caused by his physical departure from the stage of audit reform by making their own contributions to discussions on what the future can and should hold for the profession – and which, in turn, can help to ensure that its impact is fruitful, refreshing and enlightening, both intellectually and practically.

Notes

1 www.icaew.com/insights/viewpoints-on-the-news/2023/nov-2023/badenoch-outlines-frcs-new-remit
2 For a summary of this resetting of the UK government's approach to corporate governance, see https://capitalmarketsindustrytaskforce.com/wp-content/uploads/2023/11/Resetting-the-UKs-approach-to-corporate-governance-%E2%80%93-an-open-letter-from-CMIT.pdf.
3 FRC revises UK Corporate Governance Code 22 January 2024.

4 www.accountancyage.com/2023/12/15/frcs-competition-efforts-fall-flat-as-big-four-continue-to-dominate/#:~:text=Audit%20market%20share&text=However%2C%20in%202022%2C%20the%20Big,now%20audited%20by%20challenger%20firms
5 www.frc.org/documents/Plan_and_Budget_2024-25.pdf
6 https://icaew.com/technical/economy/manifesto_2024
7 https://iaasb.org/ISAforLCE

For Product Safety Concerns and Information please contact our EU representative GPSR@taylorandfrancis.com
Taylor & Francis Verlag GmbH, Kaufingerstraße 24, 80331 München, Germany

www.ingramcontent.com/pod-product-compliance
Ingram Content Group UK Ltd.
Pitfield, Milton Keynes, MK11 3LW, UK
UKHW021708230325
456549UK00023B/132

* 9 7 8 0 3 6 7 2 2 2 2 1 5 *